Red Right Returning

Hirondelle

Red Right Returning

Joan Eyolfson Cadham

Shoreline

Red Right Returning
Copyright Joan Eyolfson Cadham 1998

Cover illustration by Gilles Archambault
Photographs property of the author

Printed in Canada by AGMV Marquis, Quebec

Published by Shoreline, 23 Ste-Anne, Ste. Anne de Bellevue,
    Quebec, Canada H9X 1L1. Phone/fax 514-457-5733
    <bookline@total.net>   www.total.net/~bookline

Dépôt légal: Bibliothèque nationale du Québec and
    The National Library of Canada

Catalogue in Publication Data

Cadham, Joan Eyolfson, 1940-
    Red right returning

ISBN 1-896754-06-6

    1. Cadham, Joan Eyolfson, 1940- 2. Cadham, Jack.
3. Sailboat living. 4. Sailing--Ontario. 5. Sailing--Quebec
(Province) I. Title.

GV810.92.C33A3 1998 797.1'24'0922713 C98-900358-2

To my beloved Skipper, John Harold (Jack) Cadham,
Sept. 9, 1917 -- Oct. 21, 1995,
to the memories of long, silly summers,
and
to *Hirondelle,*
the boat we both loved.

CONTENTS ~~~~~~~~~~~~~~~~~~~~~~~~~~~~

RED? RIGHT? RETURNING? ~~~~~~~~~~~~~~~~~~

Jack preferred to travel at night. A sailor with a heart that was designed for the Pacific Ocean, he had learned to live with a boat and a budget that confined him to the local inland waterways. In turn, he made adventures out of finding his way in the dark.

My obligation was to spot the buoys. In the early eighties, we were still using the Lateral system of buoyage, green to mark off the safe port-hand side of the channel and red to mark the safe starboard hand when the boat was travelling inland, heading home, as in Red, Right, Returning. In the dark, the slender green flat-topped cylinders that marked small craft channels turned black and disappeared. So, for that matter, did the pointy-topped red ones. Finding buoys was half concentration, half miracle. I protected my night vision with a passion bordering on obsession.

One night, early in the relationship that became the permanent duo of the Skipper and the Viking First Mate, we rounded Dowker's Island off Baie d'Urfé at midnight. As I frantically searched for invisible buoys in black shadows in a winding channel, I asked Skipper, "What would happen if we hit one of these under power?"

The next morning, in full sunshine, without another boat around, just off the Senneville Yacht Club, heading west for the TransCanada Bridge and Lake of Two Mountains, Skipper plowed *Hirondelle* straight into a red buoy.

Long after we had repainted the hull and touched up the bruises in the rub rail, Jack always maintained that, like any good skipper, he was just giving his crew a practical answer to a direct question.

OVER THE BOUNDING MAIN ~~~~~~~

I think I know how to put divorce lawyers out of business. All couples considering marriage should be forced, by law, to spend three weeks alone together on a small leaky wooden sailboat in the rain. The couples that survive will be ready to weather whatever pleasant or nasty surprises that life has in store.

The original game plan when Jack and I started dating in 1980 was that, as two adults with very little in common, we would maintain a casual friendship based on skiing, sailing and a common interest in books. He was 63 and I was 40. He thrived on physical activity, mostly skiing and sailing. My favourite sport was attending Expos baseball games at the Big Owe. I thrived on long late night philosophical discussions. He taught me to ski and tried to teach me to live by his lifetime training that "nice" people didn't ever discuss politics or religion or any subject that might be genuinely meaningful for them. I discovered I liked skiing, but I was the product of an activist family. I needed to argue politics in the same way I needed oxygen.

Cruising on a little sailboat forced us together in situations where neither of us could easily escape. I thought I was getting exercise and fresh air. Jack thought he was guaranteeing a sailing companion. However, there was more going on aboard that small craft over eleven summers than just some sailing, cooking and swimming. Jack and I, under the safe guise of our roles as Skipper and First Mate, were developing our own recipes for survival together through some stormy and variable winds.

My theory about cramming couples onto little boats? It worked for us.

As romances go, Jack's and mine was wandering about, as direc-
tionless as a sailboat tacking into variable head winds - until
spring arrived and he introduced me to his 48-year-old wooden
sloop, the *Hirondelle.* I fell in love - with the boat, not with him.
(He made the love list later.)

It wasn't long, as slave to *Hirondelle,* before I learned that
an indispensable First Mate had to be able to scrape, sand, paint
and varnish, had to be able to assume pretzel-like contortions in
order to brush a protective coat onto the inner workings of the
tiny bench that some insane designer had grandly labelled "the
3/4 berth," had to be able to wear paint-streaked hair as a badge
of honour, had to understand the absolute necessity of nine
coats of varnish on all the brightwork.

He, it turned out, had never had the combination of a live-
aboard boat, lots of available time, a little spare money, and a
partner crazy enough to believe that three weeks on a slightly
leaky wooden sailboat could rate as the ultimate experience.

He never really understood my point of view. He worked in
construction, with sheets of drafting paper and cost estimates
that obeyed his dictates. Life, as he saw and lived it, was an or-
derly, organized progression. I was a single parent with three
teens of my own and den mother to various other teens who
lived with us at equally various times. I worked shift work with
emotionally disturbed preteens in a residential treatment setting.
It suited me. I thrived on chaos. However, dealing with varnish
that didn't unstick itself while I was away was the only assurance
I had, some days, that the world was unfolding as it should.

The Skipper and the Viking - an odd combination, but it
seemed to be an ordained match. By the end of the first summer,
long before I passed my own Basic Boating exam and had been
officially sworn in as a member, Jack had me actively involved
with Canadian Power and Sail Squadrons, a volunteer organisa-
tion dedicated to teaching and promoting safe boating.

Meanwhile, by fall, he had given up most forms of life-
activity except for work, CPS and navigation courses. I juggled
the intricacies of shift work with family, some other volunteer
obligations, Expos baseball games, my boating courses, and, occasionally, sleep. The winter was filled with wind songs - where
to, how to - stories of couples who had forsaken it all for one

another, a boat, a quantity of charts and the open sea. In our spare time, we did a little downhill skiing - propping ourselves up on a pile of pillows in our ski motel at day's end, reading cruising yarns.

In the spring, we scraped and painted, talked about modifications, spent most of our time on cosmetic work, organized a tiny functional galley, made summer plans to putter around the Thousand Islands and the Rideau Canal.

We never quite made the leap from Seaway to open sea. Our bookshelves, after all, held as many books about building boats, rebuilding boats, maintaining old boats and repairing battered boats as they did off-shore cruising. And, truth be known, our ancient wooden boat with the low-slung open cockpit was not designed for big seas.

We did find time, in December 1984, to get married. Somewhere around paint pots and tape measures, sail changes and late evening snacks, we had, somewhat to our mutual surprise, unapologetically fallen in love.

Our free time together fell into some sort of pattern. Spring - sand, scrape, repair, paint, and varnish. Summer - launch and spend every available hour on the boat. Autumn - put off hauling *Hirondelle* until the last minute, usually bedding her down in a sleet storm. Winter - take boating courses, teach boating courses, read boating books, ski when we could, and wait for spring.

One morning, much to our surprise, we realized there were other things to do besides sailing boats, working on boats, talking about boats, taking boating courses, going to boat shows and reading books about boating. I began to write for publication and he took stained glass courses. We travelled out west to visit family and to ski Banff.

We developed "two-foot-itis" backwards - our boats got smaller rather than bigger. He built me a 12-foot sailing craft with a carved mahogany dragon on the prow. We bought another old wooden boat - a planked St. Lawrence F class sloop that required hours of patient repair. He fitted planks and I learned to use caulking cotton.

I burned out of child care and determined to write for a living. He swung in and out of periods of retirement so that we could continue to eat while I switched to part time and continued to write. All of our kids got married. Our 21-year-old cat, she

11

who had taught Jack how to become a proper slave to the species, quietly and gracefully vanished. We decided that full-time writing alternating with intense periods of burn-out wasn't as productive as it might be.

We moved across the country, exchanging traffic jams on Lake St. Louis and the Thousand Islands for clean beaches on an almost empty little lake in Saskatchewan where sailboats were a novelty.

In 1990, we discovered that Jack had cancer. On October 21, 1995, my Skipper left on his final great voyage.

There are still wind songs. They just sing a slightly different tune.

Hirondelle at 25 de l'Eglise, Ste. Anne de Bellevue

INTERLUDE ~~~~~~~~~~~~~~~~~~~~~~~~~~~~~~~~~

Sunshine Fruit Salad was the first recipe developed to facilitate life on board *Hirondelle*

This recipe for small boat living was perfected in the late eighties and the early nineties, before all the ozone began to wear away and the sun became cruel and hot. Making this recipe regularly is still the only way to survive long periods on board, but lounging in the sun now requires a broad-brimmed cotton hat, a layer of sunscreen and at least an Indian cotton cover-up.

This fruit salad requires a perfect, lazy, sunny day when you need an excuse to loaf around in the cockpit. "I'm making fruit salad for supper," you will retort whenever anyone suggests you do anything taxing that will move you away from your book. Once they've tasted this, no one will ever again argue your right to make it.

Incidentally, in my world, "not peeled" applies only to organically grown fruit or well-washed regular stuff. I've never felt that pesticide residue adds anything to the flavour of fruit salad.

Note: The combination of the sun and the honey seems to draw the juices from the fruits, combining them, creating liquid ambrosia. The orange juice keeps the apples from turning brown. Except for the honey and the oranges, all ingredients are exchangeable.

For subtle flavour changes, try making this with a variety of Canadian honeys - cloves, wild flower, saskatoon. Buckwheat honey will overpower the flavour of some of the milder fruits.

SUNSHINE FRUIT SALAD

one perfect sunny day
3/4 cup (175 mL) honey
2 oranges
2 apples, washed, not peeled
2 plums, washed, not peeled

2 nectarines, washed, not peeled
1/2 cup (125 mL) dates
1/2 cup (125 mL) raisins
6 dried figs
unsalted pecans or cashews
    (optional)

Align yourself, your ingredients, peelers, knives, garbage bag, good book, tape recorder, a couple of your favourite audio tapes, and a big bowl in a warm sunny spot in your boat's cockpit.

Ladle the honey into the big bowl. Peel the oranges and chop them into small pieces. Work over the bowl so you don't waste any juice. Licking your fingers is encouraged.

At a very leisurely pace, wash and core the apples. Chop or slice and drop the apple pieces into the honey-orange mixture. Stir well to coat the apple pieces.

Assume the serious loafing position.

Eventually, wash and chop the other fresh fruit. Add to the mixture in the bowl and, always, stir well to coat the new fruit.

Between adding fruit to the salad, address the new book, or the music, or simply sit and enjoy the scenery.

About an hour before serving, chop the dates and the figs. Add them with the raisins. Don't add them earlier because they darken the rich juice that forms as the fruit sun-cooks in the honey.

Just before serving, sprinkle the nuts on top.

Serve sun-warm, in big bowls.

This will serve 4 or 5 people, but if there are only two of you, have the rest for breakfast with baking powder biscuits or slices of soda bread.

Before putting away leftovers, fish out and discard any fragments of nuts which will go soft and awful overnight.

FIRST ENCOUNTERS ~~~~~~~~~~~~~~~~~~~~~~~~

I met *Hirondelle* officially on April 12, 1980. She was tucked up dry in M. Levak's boathouse in Lachine, as handy as possible to the Dragon House Chinese Cafe which became a second home to the Skipper and the Viking Deckhand. The boat was painted black, which, in my estimation at least, gave her a foreshortened look, and some fool previous owner had covered her beautiful mahogany rub rails with purple imitation mahogany paint.

She had been christened *Hirondelle*, French for "barn swallow," and Skipper believed changing a boat's name was unlucky. Anyway, it suited her. Our only problem, ever, was convincing unilingual English ears in Ontario that, although they heard us say "*Ear-on-dell*," we spelled the boat's name with an *H*. That situation did arise regularly on our marine band radio.

She was a Duet class sloop, one of three built in Verdun in the late forties or early fifties from a 1946 Long Island design by Harrison Farrell. She was 23-1/2 feet LOA, 18'4" LWL, beam 7'6" and drew 27 inches with centreboard up. She could float in a bathtub and slip into and out of interesting places with a minimum of fuss. Skipper tended to stretch the half foot in the other direction and describe her as "24 feet." Knowing that the half-foot provided barely enough room for the anchor, I called her a "23-foot boat." We never did resolve that difference in perception or in bragging rights.

She had a full-length keel with 400 pounds of lead ballast and her inside ballast was a complement of lead elevator weights. Her total weight was 3500 pounds. According to Skipper, her finest asset was a 16-horse Palmer International inboard engine, his pride and joy.

She was wooden of course, marine plywood hull, with lots of mahogany trim and bright brass lettering.

Skipper had bought her in 1978. According to the way he told it, he went to Boulanger Yacht in Lachine to buy an anchor for his 18-footer, and the Danforth he bought had *Hirondelle* attached to it. He always considered her a special gift. She was his dream boat, all the boat he ever really wanted, and she cost him $400. That wonderful little engine was seized when he bought the boat. He paid to have that rebuilt, but the price was still, as he always maintained, nothing short of a miracle.

The previous owner had run out of money and Boulanger was prepared to sell the boat to recoup storage costs. She'd been in dry dock too long and needed some work. That situation, a problem for some people, simply defined *Hirondelle* even more definitely as Jack's perfect boat. He was regularly accused of preferring to work on wooden boats rather than sailing on them. Maybe. Maybe not. At any rate, by the spring of 1980, he had spent a long time working on *Hirondelle* and not much time sailing her.

Jack had learned to sail a canoe on the Delta Marshes in Manitoba when he was twelve years old. He was allowed to run before the wind but the adults in his life gave him orders to paddle back. They didn't want him trying to beat into the wind, not realizing, perhaps, that he was probably in more danger from strong winds behind than he was with the canoe heeling over.

He'd had a sailboat of some description most of his life and, by the time I met him, had discovered Canadian Power and Sail Squadrons and was happily obsessed with taking boating courses and following, to the letter, all the boating laws and traditions ever written by any navy or boating fraternity.

My first sailing ventures had been in Cold Lake, Alberta, in an un-named black homemade fibreglass outrigger canoe with a sail that I had sewed on a rented Singer zigzag sewing machine. We - my first sailing partner and our three little kids - moved to Quebec and acquired a 33-foot Chariot-class day-sailing plywood trimaran. I named her the *Astra*. She had been built in Cold Lake by a friend, and was an interesting vessel with a 13-foot beam - the ultimate floating party platform.

My first sailing partner believed that only sissies ever used the roller reefing, a conviction that led, more than once, to a broken mast. Given that only sissies carried anchors or motors, the de-mastings became adventures. The same sailor thought marine charts were cheat sheets and used the *Astra's* centreboard as a depth finder. When it shattered, it meant that we were in shallow, rocky shoal water.

Because we were going through centreboards like cold victims go through paper tissues, he began to carve them out of plywood in batches, without taking time to fibreglass them. Eventually, one splintered and jammed. He dove under to bang it free, taking along the anchor, which we had finally acquired, as a handy hammer. As the anchor headed for the bottom, as anchors are intended to do, he realized that, as usual, he had not made it fast to any part of the boat. Such was an average outing.

Fortunately, all of this happened in the early sixties, when there wasn't much pleasure craft traffic on Lake St. Louis and, because we didn't have a motor, we weren't out much after dark.

To give him his due, he has since take the CPS course and, to the best of my knowledge, still sails and no longer breaks

16

masts. I hear he also lowers anchors, hand over hand, rather than swinging them out, Olympic hammer throw fashion, and he can and will read a chart.

Still, given that my original boating adventures also included three very little children and the necessity of carrying everything on and off board every trip, my sailing memories were a jumble of contradictions. I had loved the *Astra* in the abstract. I remembered actual sailing ventures with considerably less pleasure. I have never been overly fond of roughing it, and the *Astra,* for all her beauty, came with a huge open cockpit and no conveniences. The bathroom was a bucket. The fellows simply went forward. My work surface and table was either of the two built-in bench seats. We didn't even have a camping stove.

By the time Jack introduced me to *Hirondelle*, it had been ten years since I had been on or around a sailboat and I had long forgotten the little I had learned about the art of sailing. According to my own perception, I was a fairly uncoordinated intellect, not an athlete. My idea of adventure was to play "Risk" with my kids until 4 a.m. when I knew I had to be at work for 7. My idea of recreation was dinner out, followed by live theatre or classical music.

I took one look at *Hirondelle* in a semi-dark old boathouse and fell in love, unreasonably and illogically. Equally illogically, within half an hour of meeting the boat, I let myself be introduced to Jack's sander. While I applied it to the hull, Jack vanished to buy supplies. I had never used power tools. I was suddenly alone with a boat that I didn't know and a piece of machinery that frightened me.

Three days later, Jack developed a sore throat and took to his bed. Each day, around shifts and my other obligations, I drove from Ste. Anne de Bellevue to Mr. Levak's boatyard, fired up the sander, and, obligingly, continued working alone.

Seventeen years later, it seems like madness. At the time, it seemed like perfectly normal behaviour. Working with emotionally disturbed kids is akin to living on an emotional roller coaster. The boatyard was an adventure and the waves rolling in from the lake were soothing. The boat - as soon as I convinced Jack to paint her white - was going to be beautiful. I was helping to make a difference. Besides, it was a great way to get a tan in those glorious days when we still had an ozone layer, and Mr. Levak, who by then was in his late eighties, and who had never

17

seen a girl in love with a boat before, visited me every day, offering equal doses of daily praise, advice and encouragement. It was a heady combination.

Five days later, when the Skipper finally got off the sick list and came back to the boat, he was so impressed that he took the Deck Hand home and fed her curried chicken over Basmati rice with side dishes of chopped cashews and mango chutney.

It was a successful meal. Jack had discovered curry in India during World War II. I had discovered curry through international college friends in Ste. Anne de Bellevue. Learning how to make curry on board from canned ingredients became one of my obsessions. I finally found a solution.

By then, the nicknames had become as much a part of boating life as the sails and the rigging.

Jack had lived in the Laurentians and taught skiing. He enjoyed it, and felt he did a competent job. However, by the time we met, he was feeling much less competent about his achievements in the business world. He had not lived up to his own expectations. Eventually, he realized that he was a product of circumstance - his Dad had died when Jack was only two and a half, the great Depression arrived while he was in his teens and the war claimed the first flush of manhood. He should, he realized, have gone to university and become an architect. It wasn't going to happen.

In charge of his boat, he had a purpose, a certain status by his understanding. As Skipper, he was not just another draftsman/project manager working for a succession of subcontractors.

He needed labels. He dubbed me the Viking. My Icelandic heritage fascinated him, maybe because of the seafaring connection. I didn't mind. Used on the boat, the two names, the Skipper and the Viking, gave us new identities. The Viking could be much more self-assured, much more daring than the child-care worker could. With my new name, I won the right to try to live up to the image of those early Norse.

Incidentally, I also won the right to strip all that hideous purple paint off the mahogany rub rails and to caress the wood back to life with fine grade sandpaper. I learned how to apply nine coats of varnish, sanding between coats. There were probably more useful jobs that I could have done, but I still cherish the memory of the lovely days during which I discovered

18

the satiny feel of well-treated mahogany. And Skipper was enchanted to discover that his favourite Viking matched his obsession for the feel of good wood.

My encounter with those rub rails made a positive and lasting impression. Very positive. So we were married, at Christmas, so as not to interfere with boating season.

SURVIVING THE FIRST CRUISE~~~~~~~~~~~~~~~~

We made fast below the Kingston Mills locks. I put on the kettle and dropped in a sodden heap. My entire system suddenly recognized and accepted fatigue, terminal backache, and arms that were stretched at least two inches longer than they'd been when we left Ste. Anne de Bellevue. Around the edges of my bathing suit, I could feel the itchy residue of last week's sunburn. It was compounded by a prize case of windburn.

Skipper suggested I go to bed.

A cup of tea helped. I decided a celebration supper was in order, topped off with my secret fruit salad recipe. I took some photos, stretched, and, as I dug ingredients out of the port locker, I announced that I felt like a survivor. In retrospect, it was an odd observation. I was supposed to be on holiday, having fun.

In six days, we had set sail from our yacht club, made some repairs, gone through the old Ste. Anne's locks, crossed Lake of Two Mountains, hurried up the Ottawa River, taken down the mast, motored 18 miles and made passage through 49 locks of the Rideau Canal system.

We'd managed to live on a 23-foot sailboat with her 33-foot wooden mast balanced the length of the boat, with stays, shrouds and spreaders in constant attack position. I'd learned why my Viking ancestors wore protective helmets.

Tomorrow, we would do the last five miles of the waterway, get the mast up, and prepare to sail from Kingston back to Montreal.

Tonight we were in possession of that rare gift, the key to the lock bathrooms. Just before we left Montreal, Skipper had completed a holding tank, to make *Hirondelle* legal in Ontario waters. We hadn't tested the holding tank for leaks and both of us were paranoid. We sometimes felt we'd made the cruise from lock bathroom to lock bathroom.

Later that evening, I took the usual stroll. The fireflies lit my path along the last four locks. The turning basin was mirror calm. Clover fragrance dominated the night air and hollyhocks bloomed around the lockmaster's house. *Hirondelle* waited for me, gleaming white against the trees, a tangle of halyards and lines tumbled across the deck, anticipating tomorrow's sorting and organizing. With any luck, the mast would go up more easily than it had come down, a process that had finally required the combined brute force of six young men who offered to take the place of the winch mechanism that proved to work only in theory.

No more than a thousand mosquitoes attended my return to the boat. I hadn't listened to a news broadcast or read a paper in five days. I rather figured that, if the world had stopped, some passing boater would have told us.

The Rideau had suited me, even though, concerned about time, and locked into Skipper's two-week Construction Holiday, the final two full weeks of July, we had pushed too hard at the busiest time of year. This was the season of the ritual annual exodus, two weeks when, apparently, everyone else in Quebec who was locked into Construction Holidays jumped into a boat and headed west up the Seaway to the Thousand Islands.

We had spent most of the spring working on the boat. When we did finally arrive at launch day, we also arrived at the next problem. I worked shift work, two weekends out of every three. Jack worked weekdays, 9 to 5, commuting across Montreal. He lived in Lachine. I lived in Ste. Anne de Bellevue. It wasn't easy to find time for sailing together.

I had worked alone, preparing *Hirondelle* for launch day. I wasn't about to spend time alone with her once she was launched. In fact, after 150 hours of hard, patient, painstaking work, I ended my May 24 entry in the yellow coil-bound Hilroy that became known as "Crew's Rough Log" with this comment: "When she hits the water next Monday, ready for sailing, I shall turn her back to him - for she is his. All I own is the memory of these two months, the memory of a boat, and a job to do."

We had been out sailing a few times before we left on our first cruise. However, I was still incompetent as a crew and unsure at the helm under sail, a situation compounded by a flawed depth perception, so that I white-knuckled through docking and working in close quarters. As the helmsman, Skipper was driven compulsively to nursing extra fractions of knots of speed from *Hirondelle*. Crewing for him meant having to be on constant call for sail changes. It might have been exciting had I had any idea what I was doing. It certainly wasn't relaxing.

For a sailboat to cruise through the Rideau Waterway, the mast has to come down. Ottawa boasts some beautiful old low bridges.

Once the mast came down, Crew was on holiday. When Skipper was at the helm, there was nothing to do but read, write, take photos, loaf around in the cockpit, make tea or pour the occasional juice. Taking a shift on the tiller meant drifting slowly from buoy to buoy, no pressure, no challenge, not much to do but enjoy the scenery and laugh at the antics of the ducks we startled. Occasionally we met another boat but, given a legal speed limit of nine knots, there was no wash to battle. We met, waved, separated.

There were no phones. There were absolutely no demands for quick decision and quicker action. For the first time in years, I owned my own time.

By the end of the Rideau cruise, we hadn't solved some of our more serious problems, including Skipper's need to press forward every day, scoring nautical miles like merit marks on a badge of honour, his restless need to be underway by 6 a.m. regardless of weather, lined up against my desperate need to unwind from too many years on a high-stress job, to drift, to read, to sleep. We hadn't resolved Skipper's honest conviction that if I stayed up to read with the cabin light on, I'd run down the battery and the motor wouldn't start the next morning. We hadn't resolved the ultimate dilemma, that Skipper liked eggs in the morning, for breakfast, and I liked eggs in the evening, for dinner.

However, neither of us had stalked off the boat in a fit of pique and neither of us had, yet, become an anchor. In six days, we had learned more about one another, about how we fought, and about how well we worked together in real emergencies than some couples manage in sixty years.

I lit another mosquito repellent coil, set it in the protective aluminum foil pie plate so that it would burn all night, blew a kiss at the back pedalling mosquitoes, and went to bed, appreciatively sniffing the subtle celebratory fragrance of good curry.

There is no better potpourri for an old, slightly damp wooden boat than the lingering fragrance of cumin, coriander and garam masala.

IN THE BEGINNING ~~~~~~~~~~~~~~~~~~~~~~~~~~~~~

For the innocent on shore, the sight of a 24-foot sailboat, sails drawing, gleaming white with freshly varnished brightwork and a jaunty red waterline, silently slipping across the lake, conjures up images of below-deck elegance and glamorous living.

The truth is, sometimes, somewhat unlike the fantasy.

Hirondelle's cockpit was 6' 6". The pointy bit at the bow was too narrow to hold much but sail bags and the anchor. There were also bits at the stern that were not usable living space. That left, according to the designer's own specs, eleven feet of living space below decks, on a beam of 8' 6".

The beam width wasn't the cabin width. There did have to be space all around the cabin for Crew to make mad dashes forward for sail changes and anchor lowering or raising. And the 8' 6" measured the widest spot. On the curved sides of a pleasure craft, that measurement shrinks fairly quickly.

So, what did we have? The high point of the cabin, the 4' 6" headroom, was over the galley - four feet of space about six feet across, an area that included the galley and Crew's quarters with a small bench, a work table, and room for Crew's note books, portable typewriter and large camera bag as well as the Navigator's tools and charts. The head (nautical for bathroom) was 20 inches wide and maybe two feet long. Across from the head was the hanging locker (closet) which held both our foul weather gear and our two good outfits, reserved for church, theatre and dining out in style.

The head was wider than the hanging locker. That measurement cut down on the length of the First Mate's bunk. Her bunk was 5' 4" by the designer's own specs. Skipper's was about four inches longer. He claimed it on the grounds that he was both taller and older. Both bunks were 27 inches wide, a little narrower than a baby's crib.

Headroom in the bedroom was 3' 6".

The sales brochure - now at least 50 years old - gaily talks about "a little auxiliary sloop that starts you thinking of distant ports and the lure of new waters. Perhaps," the sales pitch continues, "it's because such a craft is designed to 'live at sea' and seems to say: 'Let's go, boss - the ice chest is full, there's gas in the tank, the bunks are made up and the breeze is freshening'."

Duet, insists the ad writer, "is indeed guilty of such captivation and persuasiveness, with four inside berths, an enclosed toilet, hanging locker, complete galley, and a big cockpit ... her cabin is unusually roomy."

I don't know who made these claims or whether he ever spent three weeks aboard a Duet-class sailboat. He only got one thing right. He said, "Duet attracts favourable comment wherever seen and has gained the admiration of cruising enthusiasts everywhere." He was right. Everyone recognized our little boat and everyone admitted she was the prettiest thing on the water. And she was, even though we lived in a crouch below decks, even though we backed into the head, even though I never did understand where the designer would suggest we might have built the other two bunks.

I often wonder what other craft of the era offered.

But, have you ever seen anyone in love? The flaws - even the obvious ones - presented by the love object don't matter. Love is, indeed, blind. We were in love, undoubtedly. Both Skipper and First Mate were madly in love with *Hirondelle,* and, truth be known, with one another. Some of the best days of our lives were spent in that big open cockpit. Some of our best meals came out of that tiny galley. And some of our best nights were spent in those 27-inch bunks.

LET'S GET ORGANIZED ~~~~~~~~~~~~~~~~~~~~~~~

An east wind was heaping waves against a westerly current, neither of us had managed much sleep, and we finally decided that, while upping anchor and wallowing to the nearest marina under motor would be more adventure than either of us wanted at 5 a.m., at least there would be a guarantee of sleep when we arrived. Sleep at our present anchorage on the windward side of a little island was not going to happen.

We struggled into Brockville in deteriorating weather about 8 a.m. As we gratefully made fast, we watched a family of four spill out of their car and onto the dock.

The husband and his sons romped off to their boat, visiting along the way, leaving the wife to stagger back and forth three or four times, laden down with boxes, clothes, hampers, bedding, and sundry other packages. She stopped briefly to ask my opinion of the day's weather.

"Interesting," I suggested, trying to be as diplomatic as possible now that Skipper and I had decided to sleep, read, drink tea and take ourselves out later to dine elegantly at a real table that wasn't going to move around.

"I hate sailing," she responded. "I'd rather be home cutting the grass."

I made some mental notes about the possible relationship between her husband and various members of the canine family.

And then I wondered about the wisdom of spending $30,000 on a boat but being too cheap to buy two can openers and two sets of paring knives, a spare set of pillowcases, and a tea towel, so that one set could remain on board all summer long.

On the *Astra*, the captain and I had carted everything - including three very small people - on and off every trip. I always forgot some essential. I have developed a permanent aversion to buns without butter, eggs without salt, and picnic coolers awash in half-melted ice cubes grinding against little floating bits of butter, congealed bacon fat and the cheese I thought I had sealed in a waterproof bag. It was camping out at its worst.

Jack had also done his share of camping-out sailing, some of which he had quite enjoyed. However, by the time he and I realized that we should get married and sail happily ever after, we had had lots of time to compare boating horror stories and to

24

sort out our mutual bits of philosophy regarding cruising sail-boats.

We knew that, if we really required luxurious accommodations and full-sized modern well-appointed kitchens, we would not be drifting around in a small boat. I categorized "small boat" as anything afloat under about 250 feet. Skipper disagreed - he maintained he would have felt un-cramped on about 100 feet. On the other hand, no one was going to give us a medal for running *Hirondelle* with all the comfort and convenience of a 16th-century slave ship.

We weren't going to buy a bigger boat. We couldn't afford one and, besides, we were hopelessly attached to the lady *Hirondelle*. We tried to find ways to make our small spaces as efficient and cozy as possible The first requirement, we decided very quickly, was to have all necessities permanently on board. But, with the boat, there was the added question of what to do about the galley.

According to my *Canadian Edition Collins Dictionary*, a galley is: a one-decked vessel with sails and oars, usually rowed by slaves or criminals. Having said that, *Collins* continues with a second definition: kitchen of ship. A galley slave is one condemned to row in a galley. The Eyolfson Cadham extra definition is: to cook in one.

Hirondelle's galley was tucked into four feet of space starboard of the companionway. Even "galley" was a grand word for a two-burner alcohol stove, a tiny sink, three small drawers, a few cup hooks, and a two-foot by two-foot open storage space. There was no standing headroom for a cook who was taller than four feet tall and I happen to be 22 inches taller than four feet.

Even so, the galley had come a long way since my first introduction. That close look came after several weeks of being permitted to sand, scrape, varnish and otherwise minister to *Hirondelle's* rather elderly hull. At first sight, the galley was not a promising situation. Every inch of the limited drawer and locker space was crammed with cleats, cams, brass screws, clevis pins, turnbuckles, blocks and line, Skipper's collection of absolutely essential spares.

The galley did offer a two-burner un-gimballed propane stove and a tiny gravity-fill sink that would have functioned had there been any water in the tank and if the sink hadn't also become storage space for spares. There was also a portable "galley box" that held a sterno stove, a jar of questionable rice, some rock-hard salt, and two tins of potatoes.

To facilitate cooking, serving and eating, Skipper had bought a cunning collection of soft plastic dishes and cups which cleverly fit around some very tiny aluminum pots. The entire contraption was held together with a carrying handle secured with a pair of wing nuts. Two years later, I finally put the carrying handle to good use - I trotted dishes, cups, pots and handle off the boat and got rid of them.

Skipper claimed to live on apples, hard cheese, pepperoni and canned soup. I believed him.

We had been concluding our work sessions with Chinese food at Dragon House - the management didn't mind watching us dive for the bathrooms and hot water so that we could remove three or four layers of paint and varnish. By the time we dried off and met at our favourite table, there would be a pot of Jasmine tea waiting for us.

It was a wonderful tradition-in-the-making, but I had a point to make. I might be about as subtle as a falling concrete block, but I get results. One bright afternoon, on one of my weekday days off, I made it to the boathouse, as usual, well in advance of Jack. Unlike other days, I knocked off sanding early. With not a little concern, I fired up the sterno stove, and, by the time Jack arrived, I was ready - with those little orange plastic plates - to serve him a simple meal of ham in raisin sauce complemented with steamed rice and topped off with fresh strawberries dipped in sugar and drowned in cream. After Skipper had licked up the last of the cream, I suggested that if I were to sign aboard *Hirondelle* as Galley Slave, Cabin Girl, Ship's Cook or First Mate, there would be some changes made.

Skipper had the good grace to know when he was bested. Out went the cleats, the blocks and the screws. In came the pots, the dishes and the spices, and for the next eleven summers, we took turns cooking for one another - which, sometimes when the moon is full and the wind is gentle, leads me to wonder who was actually had.

I had just mastered the on-board propane stove when Jack invited the insurance agent to inspect the boat. The agent was not impressed with the propane installation. He told us that to have the boat insured in Canada would require either an involved and space-consuming installation or the propane had to go. We decided *Hirondelle* had no extra space to offer. Out went the propane, replaced by a two-burner pressurized alcohol stove with a vicious tendency to run out of fuel two-thirds of the way through boiling potatoes. It was slow, and would not cook "hot."

Neither of us enjoyed cooking on a barbecue. We carried a small one for a couple of years until we realized it had gotten wet and rusted. We took it home, thinking we might use it there. We didn't. There was no real reason why we didn't like the barbecue - except that maybe both of us were too impatient to wait until coals were right for cooking.

As a result, we were dependent on the alcohol stove. We never managed a decent steak on it, and I realize now that we would have been further ahead to update the propane installation. However, we didn't, and the monster stove and I learned to co-exist.

But galley life wasn't all drudgery. In fair weather, I could sit comfortably on the top companionway step with the hatch cover pushed back and my head in the fresh air, and putter contentedly with everything I needed literally within fingertip reach. I was, in fact, always grateful that the galley was at the aft-end of the cabin and not amidships where I would have felt quite claustrophobic.

Skipper loved his pressure cooker and used it all the time. On shore, in our kitchen, I loved to know he was cooking up his one-pot old-fashioned specialty, pork hocks with steamed potatoes, carrots and cabbage, with lots of bay leaf and whole peppercorns. However, the pressure cooker terrified me. I knew that in my hands it would immediately explode, blowing up through our cabin roof and crashing down through the cabin roof of the nearest boat, landing directly on top of their innocently sleeping child. I didn't even want to be in the cabin when Skipper was using the pressure cooker.

A chat with our Baie d'Urfé boating friend, Berny Peissel, solved my pressure cooker problem.

"You like to cook bread and biscuits on board, don't you?" Berny asked.

Of course I did. The problem, working without an oven, was finding a pot with a thick bottom so the bread wouldn't burn. I had also given up on getting biscuits to brown on top.

Berny and Monique had cruised for years with their three boys aboard. They had developed a fair collection of their own boating tricks, including the easy way to deal with bread.

"Use the pressure cooker," Berny said.

He explained that I should discard the rocker part, and take the valve out of the lid. Now I had a really thick pot that spread heat very evenly.

The next step was to plug up the hole in the centre of the lid with a little twist of aluminum foil. If any pressure built up - which it couldn't without the rocker and the valve - the aluminum foil would blow out.

The divider or a cake rack went into the bottom of the pressure cooker so the pan of bread or buns or cake wouldn't sit directly against the heat. On went the lid. Cooking time, over medium heat, was almost identical to the baking time in a regular oven.

Voila! Worked like a charm. The biscuits even browned. In truth, disabling the pressure cooker and making a useful pot out of it was a soul-satisfying experience for me, even though pressure cooker enthusiasts would never understand.

The trick for me for good bread and biscuits was to practice at home, in a kitchen with standing headroom and lots of space and no other distractions, while I recorded cooking times.

28

In fact, over the winter, I liked to try out our boating recipes, using the boating pots which came home after haul-out for
a good hot scrubbing. Working in a kitchen with standing headroom always made experimenting a little easier. Besides, it was
one way that, during the winter, we could remind ourselves of
summer.

TRYING TO MAKE IT ALL FIT ~~~~~~~~~~~~~~~~~

From the day *Hirondelle* received her spring re-fit until that un-
happy day when she was hauled for the winter, I could plan to
stay on board for an overnight, a day, or a week with no concerns beyond whether we had any fresh reading material. I
could, if I wished, bring a bag of fresh produce, but the point
was that I didn't need it. I wouldn't put myself in the position of
having to shop for dinner each night as I come home from work.
The boat, like my home, was kept stocked with staples.

My sister Evelyn lived in the Yukon for some years. She said
the greatest challenge to survival was learning to shop six
months at a time. That's how often the supply planes came in.

I wasn't going to be away from a source of groceries for six
days at a time, but stocking the boat created our own set of
problems. I thought to keep cross-referenced indexed lists, but,
such being the nature of these items, they persisted in escaping
from their binders to slip silently through the floorboards, ultimately committing suicide to reincarnate as sodden little balls
jammed firmly up the float of the bilge pump.

So, I resorted to mental lists, regular visual checks, and strict
monitoring of the absolute essentials. I also believed in a fair bit
of flexibility in menu planning.

There was another serious consideration. I had grown up in
Saskatchewan in the forties. For various political reasons, power
poles were not run out into the farming communities until long
after the cities and towns had electricity. I lived on one of those
power-less farms and know how well people can eat without a
refrigeration unit, excepting the natural one we called "winter."

The Eyolfson Cadham theory of things mechanical runs thusly: "If it can break down, it will. The self-destruct rate of mechanical objects is directly proportional to a human's absolute reliance on that object's correct functioning."

Hirondelle did not have a mechanical refrigerator. She was built with an icebox situated under the galley stove. It was the perfect size to hold either two blocks of ice and no food, or one block of ice and a bit of food, or a bag of ice cubes and three days' worth of perishables that were all busily getting too warm because the ice cubes didn't last more than twelve hours.

When we had the boat inspected for insurance, the agent (the same one who didn't like our propane connection) suggested that, since the icebox drained directly into the bilge, we would eventually experience a soft spot in the starboard hull just below the waterline. I suspected that he was trying to say, "Keep using that thing, and the boat's going to rot out from under you."

I went sailing to run away. I didn't want to be tied to shore by an electric cord. I wanted to overnight at some quiet spot that had been chosen for beauty or romance by a committee comprised of my favourite Skipper, the Crew (that was me) and the Weatherman (that was me, too). The saddest phrases I ever heard from cruising couples went: "No, it's a beautiful anchorage, but we've got to find a marina. We need ice." Or "We can't stay there. They don't have shore power and we need to plug in."

On the other hand, I have no objection to fresh milk, cottage cheese and bacon. When we could get a block of ice or some cubes for the icebox, we did. Although we were sailors, Skipper often maintained that in lieu of a real Genoa sail, one of his best "sails" was his "Iron Genny," the 16-horse Palmer International, so we could get supplies if we wanted.

Generally speaking, it didn't take long for me to discover that I would much rather sail, laze around the deck, or read than spend hours below decks preparing meals. However, both Skipper and I enjoyed good food. We also both enjoyed cooking.

I always tried to remember that the less time we spent in the galley, the more time we had for essential chores - reading, swimming, sunning, sailing, visiting other boaters, or just holding hands, drinking tea and watching sunsets together.

Learning to shop for the boat was a slow process that evolved over several years of much trial and error. Stowage, on the other hand, was a lesson learned in one rush.

Having done a springtime shopping that nicely matched our launch date, I suggested that we berth *Hirondelle* at the Ste. Anne's canal, east of the lock, to facilitate loading.

While Jack fussed with the shrouds and stays - we always spent so much time on cosmetics that we never had time to tune the mast before we left on our first cruise - I sorted and made lists and classified busily for a couple of days. Finally satisfied, I stowed all our supplies, arranging them by long-term versus short-term use and by menu selection. By the time we cast off for a weekend shakedown cruise, I was highly impressed with my efficiency and my organization.

Before we reached the Beauharnois locks, we discovered that, along with the usual post-launch problems, we had a noticeable port-side list. Up came the floorboards. Nothing scary in the bilge. We decided to continue on to Valleyfield, on the eastern shore of Lake St. Francis. Edgy, we took turns searching for more than the normal number of leaks, trying to find some simple, logical reason why *Hirondelle* couldn't stand upright.

Once we got out into Lake St. Francis, we also learned that she could no longer point up on a starboard tack. An elderly wooden sloop with a three-quarter rig, she didn't point as well, ever, as a modern sailboat, but we were now losing on every starboard tack any ground that we had made on port tack.

We admitted the seriousness of the problem when we realized that we had just passed the same fishing boat for the third time - and he was anchored.

A visual check on the standing rigging did not reveal any problems. Skipper decided to try tightening the shrouds. We anchored so that Skipper could dig his toolbox out of the port cockpit locker - and, like magic, *Hirondelle* snapped to attention.

The galley, such as it was, was located starboard. Before I came on board, Skipper's spares had weighed down the galley drawers. The propane tank had been in the starboard locker. It had been thrown out with the propane stove. Skipper's spares had been shifted to a giant toolbox stowed in the port cockpit locker, snugged up against the newly-purchased second battery. Because access to the starboard food locker was limited by the Cook's ability to safely circumnavigate the nether portions of the

31

alcohol stove, I had put paper products and boxes here for long-term storage. All the cans had gone portside. We had taken everything heavy we could find and piled it all into four feet of stern port space. I immediately developed a new storage rule: Keep the boat balanced. Food, wherever stored, will surface as needed.

Coupled to that rule was the profound reality that, on board *Hirondelle,* anything that shouldn't get wet, did. Given half a chance, wet things spawned mildew, mould and fungus, and spread this infestation stealthily through the boat until we finally would realize that the bunks had fresh mildew spots and we would have to wage another anti-spore campaign.

BUT THERE'S MORE TO A BOAT THAN A GALLEY ~

Out of the Ile Perrot Yacht Club harbour, around the racing buoy, back into the harbour, up to our berth, pause, out of the harbour, round the racing buoy, and back in again. "Circuits and bumps," according to Skipper.

The weather had been perfect for a weekend on the boat, but meetings and appointments had chewed my time into useless little chunks. We were not going anywhere - except out of the harbour and around the buoy. It was a practice session for me, as a direct result of the PAN PAN (a marine radio message that declares urgency that isn't the MAYDAY emergency.)

We had been out on Lake St. Francis when we heard Burlington Coast Guard ring out on channel 16. It wasn't unusual - some peculiarity of the air waves often brought these distant American voices through our marine radio as though they were just a knot or two away.

"Man overboard." We both went on mental alert, although we were miles away. Then the full impact of the second half of the PAN PAN struck us.

"Person left on board cannot operate vessel."

I took a long look at my favourite Skipper and wondered how I'd feel as he went down for the third time just because I couldn't get the boat back to him.

32

I could operate *Hirondelle*. I often did. I enjoyed fighting the currents in the St. Lawrence Seaway, and I enjoyed taking over at sunset, whispering along, watching the clouds explode into rose-and-lilac fragments. But we'd fallen into a pattern of Skipper doing all the close work.

We talked to other cruising couples and discovered we weren't unique.

"My control panel looks like an airplane cockpit. She'd never figure it out."

"I'm tired after a working week, so I unload the food and do the cooking and he mans the boat."

"Person on board does not know how to operate vessel."

According to a consensus of boaters who were vacationing around Gananoque in the Thousand Islands chain one summer, the absolute basic knowledge for the crew includes stopping the boat, getting an anchor down, being able to radio for help and give a position and a usable description of the vessel, getting the boat started again, coming alongside some sort of dock, and being able to effect an in-water rescue. It was more than just taking a CPS course. It was all about practical knowledge.

I could handle all the first part. And Skipper and I had a rule that worked for us: in rough weather, he took the helm and I took the sails and the foredeck. I figured that, in a storm-induced overboard situation, he had the skills to rescue me faster than I could rescue him. There were times when it was almost more than Jack could handle to watch me bounce around a slippery deck with my arms filled with sails that required taming. He often suggested that I should take over the tiller. In most issues relating to the boat, it was faster and simpler to do it Skipper's way. This was not such an issue. Besides, I'm an entirely competent swimmer and we both wore life jackets (more correctly, PFDs, personal flotation devices) properly fitted and fastened.

However, unexpected things happen on small boats. I decided I needed some rescue practice.

We picked a day when the winds were so confused they apparently blew from all points of the compass at the same time. They were not strong winds - which would have been potentially harmful to *Hirondelle*'s paint job - but the variability forced me to think out manoeuvres for each and every landing.

Our best "man overboard" was a partly submerged plastic grocery bag. It was cheap, available, and it required some urgency in rescuing, before it sank and reappeared wrapped around somebody's propeller. I practiced turns and approaches until I could cut power and drift alongside, while Skipper "rescued" the bag which, bobbing around low in the waves, approximated a swimmer's head. This pointed out some of the challenge of keeping a victim in sight. I wanted *Hirondelle* back from her cruises with both of us safely on board. "Person on board cannot operate vessel." Not on our boat.

After our first boating season, I realized I wouldn't spend another holiday as chief "gofer." I also didn't intend to spend another holiday as chief cook and dish washer. I wouldn't presume to tell another couple how to divide up shipboard chores. That's tantamount to telling someone how to run a marriage. Skipper and I worked out our own job-sharing solutions by trial, error, and the occasional raging battle.

Jack came to our relationship with a strange view of boating life, created partly by his interpretation of a section of the CPS basic boating course, wherein it is stated that "When underway, the skipper is fully responsible for all aspects of the boat, including the following, etc., etc., etc." Jack read that as "The Skipper is in absolute control and will be obeyed absolutely." Maybe he'd read too many sea stories before he took his CPS courses.

Vikings don't take absolute orders well, and Jack did maintain I was a throwback. A mutiny was inevitable.

It came in the harbour of our yacht club. Jack wanted to adjust something and ordered me to take the helm. It was a weekend, the harbour was full of boating traffic.

I am not good at close quarters. Frankly, I can barely parallel park my truck. I have no idea where I am relative to blunt objects such as curbs or docks. The truck at least has brakes and no sideways drift. And I can stop, get out, have a look, and make corrective movements. The boat was not so forgiving.

Making a fool of myself in public is not on my "To do" list. Ever.

I refused. Jack blew up. He actually said, "You have to do it. I am the Skipper and I have given an order."

The explosion was probably heard clear to Newfoundland.

Give Jack credit. Some boating lessons did carry over to real life. Many years later, a group of Foam Lake women who needed more volunteers for their organization approached Jack with this request: "Please tell Joan that she has to join...." Jack's response, the response of an older and much wiser person, was "Sorry, but nobody tells Joan she 'has' to do anything."

The first headlong encounter with two opposing viewpoints wasn't the last. Temperamentally, we were very different people. However, when we managed to get our differences working for us, we did work together very well and enjoyed ourselves most wondrously in the process.

We both readied the boat for launching. Elderly wooden boats require a fair amount of love and hard work each spring to make them seaworthy and beautiful. Although the entire summer was spent bumping into docks and lock walls that scraped off white paint and gouged nine coats of varnish off mahogany rub rails, I happened to believe that painting cabins and sanding mahogany was great therapy. It was also a good way to get a head start on the summer tan, back when toasting a nice even brown was part of the summer ritual.

We were both affected by some rare form of spring-sun sickness that seems to strike only the owners of elderly wooden boats. The most obvious symptom was an inability to settle for a moderate amount of improvement. We would make wild plans. "Well, while you tear down the cockpit and rebuild it, I'll scrape the entire deck and cabin by hand and do three coats of paint before I start the varnishing."

We were both working full time. I had a family of teenagers who wanted and needed equal time. I also happened to enjoy their company. Jack and I never met our projected launch date.

Provisioning was divided up by expertise. Skipper handled spares, tools and hardware. I did bedding, galley and First Aid kit. We tumbled everything, including the cushions, the life jackets and the bedding, on board, then we worked at making some sort of order out of it all. I make a point of this, having had an experience in stark awareness one spring evening.

Skipper had just launched *Hirondelle*. I hadn't been well so I hadn't gone down to the yacht club. (In truth, watching the boat helplessly dangling from the end of a crane was not something I handled even when I was entirely well.) Skipper decided to take the boat on a battery-charging run to Ste. Anne's so he could pick me up and offer me a joy ride back to the club. On a pleasant, normally fifteen-minute trip, we ran out of gas about halfway to the club.

We realized, about that time, that we did not have the mast, the boom, nor any sails on board, that it was late evening, that the battery wasn't charged enough to power the running lights for any length of time, and that we were in an absolutely bare boat - no bunk mattresses, no blankets, no life jackets, no food and no warm jackets. The VHF antenna went on top the mast, so we also had no radio. I was recovering from major surgery.

We had never really considered paddling a 23-foot sailboat, but, in a pinch, Skipper could be very resourceful. Playing the little bit of current and the favourable evening breezes, he "sailed" the mast-less, sail-less craft back to the yacht club, getting one last gasp from the motor in time to tuck us up safely at an outside dock.

From that moment, life jackets, warm clothes, coffee, a can of milk and bedding were the first things on board. Some experiences just aren't worth repeating.

Skipper usually spent all his free time for the first week after the boat was launched doing last minute bits and chores, tuning the engine, tightening the shrouds, generally tinkering.

I stowed. I was much tidier aboard than I ever was at home.

The trick with one person stowing on a two-person boat is to make sure the other person knows where everything is. We settled on general areas for most things, but stores were shifted around as we got better at organizing.

Skipper was by far the more experienced sailor and did most of the sailing. In turn, I took over much of the motoring and the galley chores when we were under way. I didn't like being in the cabin in rough weather, so foul weather meals were designed to keep me out of the cabin as much as possible. I enjoyed taking the helm in rough weather more than I liked preparing meals in a tiny, motion-filled galley.

Unless he had a specific and urgent maintenance chore, Skipper was restless when he wasn't at the helm, even though he might be tired and needed a break, and I needed the experience. As a consequence, I did far less actual sailing than I should have, but, since I take on new situations in very small pieces, I suspect I didn't insist as much as I might have.

We ran on a "cook doesn't have to do dishes" arrangement. We both tidied up and we both scrubbed decks. First Mate was known for over-the-siding with a sponge in one hand and a scrub brush in her teeth to de-green the water line. Skipper generally made up the bunks because that chore generated more head bashing for the First Mate than any other, except for getting stores out of the locker that was under the stove, around the pots and over the icebox.

We operated on somewhat different principles aboard *Hirondelle* than we did at home. Why? Well, in the big old house in Ste. Anne's, we had more than ten feet of living space. Once aboard *Hirondelle*, it was a little tough to go for a brisk walk when one of us needed time-out. Neither of us ever threw the other overboard in a moment of anger - although both of us surely considered the possibility more than once.

Skipper was a morning person. I was a nighthawk. When he wasn't on holiday, Jack liked to be at work by 7:30 a.m. so that he could get a decent day's work done before the office was cluttered up by the rest of the staff. I liked to write until 3 a.m. and sleep until 10. Other than the hideously early 7 a.m.- 3 p.m. stints, I loved working shift work. Odd hours suited my rhythms. They didn't suit Skipper's natural rhythms at all.

Skipper figured that people on holidays should be under way by 6 a.m. The First Mate didn't. Skipper figured that people on holidays should be in bed by 8 p.m. to be ready for the morning. The First Mate didn't. Skipper insisted that, if the First Mate listened to classical music or, especially, Expos baseball games on the AM/FM radio - a car radio installed in the bulkhead over First Mate's bunk and powered from the battery - she would destroy the boat's power source. There were a few heated discussions, mostly generated by First Mate. Skipper perfected the silent treatment. The First Mate threatened to take a bus home. Skipper decided that, even through First Mate was unreasonable and entirely insubordinate, she was learning to make a perfect curry, legally there had to be two people on board to lock through the Seaway locks, and, besides, he would miss her.

They worked out a compromise. First Mate fussed over Skipper in the evenings, when his personal battery had run down. Skipper discovered he could stay up a little later and sleep later. He admitted he liked the classical music and he learned to tolerate First Mate's obsession with the Expos. Rather than rushing towards an early getaway, he made tea for First Mate every morning and gave her time alone to drink it, comb her hair and brush her teeth. In return, First Mate cooked bacon and eggs for Skipper, even though she does not willingly swallow eggs in the morning. Once she got Skipper fed, she ate grapefruit, peeled, pulled into segments dripping juice, and drank some more tea.

Once ashore, Jack discovered that he was locked into a morning tea routine. One of the lovely side benefits of cruising on board *Hirondelle* was that the bedside morning cup of tea appeared, hot and inviting, for as long as Jack lived. Sometimes it appeared with a basket of hot biscuits, butter and jam. I still miss it.

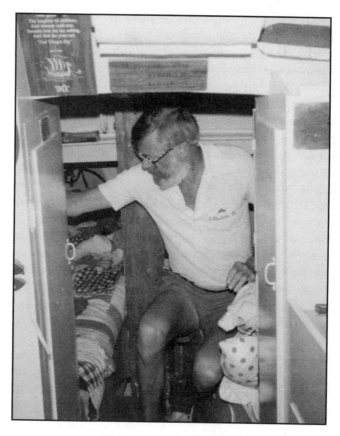

Making up the bunks

KINDRED SPIRITS ~~~~~~~~~~~~~~~~~~~~~~~~~~~

Beyond the adventure and relaxation, there are certain advantages to cruising. The finest of these is the instant, if temporary, camaraderie that springs up between cruisers who have conquered, for example, the almost impossible feat of securing the last two dock spaces at Camelot Island in the Thousand Islands chain on a Friday night. The wash of good feeling and victory forms a 14-hour bond of friendship that culminates in the invitation, "Come on over for coffee."

The first contact was Skipper's responsibility. I am an introvert. I don't do first encounters unless I am travelling in the guise of "Joan Cadham, Girl Reporter." Skipper was an extrovert with an unquenchable curiosity. He enjoyed the accidental meeting and it was toward him that the "Come on over for a drink" offers were made. Once he'd broken the ice, I could straggle along and surprise myself, each time, by fitting in and having a good time.

Undoubtedly, there is something special about cruising friendships, something that supersedes the usual polite organizing along geo-socio-politico-economic lines. I don't know where some of my boating friends work, I don't know how they vote or, indeed, whether or not they do. I don't know much about their roots. Nor, for that matter, do I care.

And, in Quebec, where there is supposed to be a language barrier, an admiring salute, a smile and a wave are bilingual. Some of our best conversations have been in "franglais." The love of cruising is a universal language.

I come from the prairies, from Saskatchewan, a province that joined Confederation in 1905, where the last of the original pioneers can still talk from personal experience about ox carts, prairie fires and the dust bowl days of the Great Depression.

There is a closeness on the prairies, a willingness to become involved, to help, to encourage, to share, that is born as much as anything from the knowledge that there is a common enemy, the weather. The wind is a friend or the enemy. Rain is a blessing or a disaster. The sun is a gift or a destroyer.

To some extent, the lives of people who choose to mess about in small boats are also controlled and ordered by self-serving, untamable forces, so that cruisers meet with a common bond already established.

And cruisers will share the oddest things with each other. They'll share their precious power tools with people they have barely met. One couple on an impressively big power cruiser invited me to drip my way over their carpet so that I could use their stern swim platform. We've towed people and been towed. We've swapped advice on everything - the best mooring spots, good places to eat in unfamiliar towns, recipes, storage tips.

We discovered we had worlds in common with Tony and Vince, teenagers who were padding the Rideau in a canoe they'd bought for $5. There was no age barrier and we had to concede something to them when they paddled from Brewers to Kingston Mills faster than we could motor in our sailboat.

We've shared barbecue coals and shopping carts and taxis into town, and pored over charts, pointing out good swimming holes and rocks to avoid, and becoming privy, in return, to romantic little anchorages and shallow-draft shortcuts.

But, most of all, the cruisers we met enjoyed getting together on a warm summer's night and, like the natives of my beloved prairies, swapping horror stories - the blow of '84, the grounding of the summer of '79, the dragging anchor of '81, all the yarns that prove the premise that it's us against the elements and that we can win.

So, I'll never be as close to another knitter or another skier, or another bridge player as I am to a sailor with whom I have shared a two-day mooring at Georgina Island.

Besides, these casual encounters often led to the sharing of solutions to some of the problems involved in cruising on small boats. I even learned tips for ways to manage in smallish spaces without doing bodily harm to self or to shipmate, either accidentally or deliberately.

On invitation, I would hungrily prowl other small craft, unashamedly asking questions, peering into likely corners, coffee cup in hand, greedily stealing all the best ideas for when and how, looking for a clever use for a storage hammock, a better place to store the ladder, ideas for a collapsible table.

Sometimes we would hunker down and philosophize for hours, working our way through a dozen topics, exploring ideas, our discussions enriched by the splash of water, the cry of a distant loon, fresh hot coffee.

Sometimes we spent an evening swapping concrete solutions to boating problems. Some magic nights, we combined the finest mix of practicality and philosophy. There is, of course, the reality of the confessional - most of us will reveal to strangers in safe, enclosed spaces, stories and attitudes that we try to shield from our friends and, often, from ourselves. The lingering benefit of those nights on other people's boats was the insights into ourselves we developed as we heard ourselves talking about our hopes, our dreams, our fears, our world concerns to strangers with whom we shared only a passion for water and small boats.

The best concise insight that I have ever heard regarding engine problems came on one such night from Louis Mandel of *Miss Moneypenny*. "I spent five years cruising before I learned this basic lesson," he said. "In an emergency, lower an anchor first. I've made all my mistakes in those first few panicky moments when I'm not sure what's wrong. With an anchor down, the boat is safe and I can address the problem logically."

One magic night, as we settled down on Georgina Island, listening to the pleasant hum of traffic from the Hill Island Bridge, Neal Price invited us for coffee aboard *Kayastar*. He had a small white cotton hammock hung from two hooks set into bulkheads in his galley and, in that hammock, swinging happily, well aired to prevent rot and wrinkles, was a crisp array of inviting fruits and vegetables.

I am a salad junkie. The first two years we cruised, I'd be in serious crisis halfway through our annual holiday. I couldn't find a space on board to keep fresh fruits and vegetables from getting scrambled, beaten or limp. I was so discouraged with the garbage I was creating that I quit carrying anything except hard apples, which I don't like, potatoes, and onions. We went hammock shopping during our next shore leave. Sometimes the ideas were so beautifully simple that I was dumbfounded I hadn't thought of them. I was agonizing over macaroni that had moulded through the cardboard box, an unpleasant surprise, and I was wondering how I could collect enough plastic containers for all the dry supplies - pastas, rice, cereals and flours. Jacques explained that, for cruising aboard *Gite*, he and his wife bought boxes that fit into large Ziploc bags. Voila! Waterproof containers.

Jack and I were both compulsive obsessive readers. We never cured a condensation problem in our old wooden boat. While the situation was not too serious in midsummer, our cabin was often decidedly damp at day's beginning in late spring and early fall. Books don't take kindly to being dripped upon. We stole a practical solution from a cruiser at Chrysler Marina. Not only did we learn to buy secondhand books, we learned how to pick the books. Most secondhand book stores sell books at half the face value. Older editions contain exactly the same number of pages and words as new editions, at a fraction of the price. They usually got mouldy or damp before the spine broke and the pages fell out.

Because *Hirondelle* was a wooden boat, we carried an assortment of bits for body repair, touch up and just plain fiddling around and feeling useful. Skipper had a compulsive need to putter. He had put in many frustrated years looking for the ideal toolbox until he discovered the answer on a boat waiting to lock through one of the Seaway locks. *Hirondelle* soon had her own big non-rusting plastic fishing tackle toolbox, filled with little compartments to hold brass screws and parts in some semblance of order, and lots of trays for tools.

My CPS Seamanship Power instructor provided the definitive answer to the type and quality of spares and tools to carry on board. Tony's rule: "Don't sink the boat with tools. Take along tools you can use to your capacity to make repairs plus any specialized equipment you might need in an emergency and that a mechanic might not have."

Jack quit smoking in 1966. I quit in 1981. We saved money and we learned to breathe with a new freedom, but we had a problem as a cruising couple. We'd meet compatible sailors along the way and discover that we didn't have the traditional half-empty cigarette pack to use for scribbling down addresses and phone numbers.

Enter the charming couple on *Old Love*, up in Gananoque. They gave us the solution over a post-swim coffee. They'd had "business" cards printed, with their boat name where a company name would be, with their names, their home address, their VHF call sign and their home phone number. Deciding that imitation was, after all, the greatest form of flattery, we had a stack of cards printed, inexpensively and quickly, that fall.

A member of Search and Rescue, Canadian Coast Guard, offered some food for serious consideration.

"Absolutely no one would take off in a car that had no air in the tires," he said. "Motorists check their oil, their gas, their antifreeze in the winter, windshield washer in the summer. They have a glove compartment full of appropriate road maps. But these same motorists have engine breakdowns on the water and they aren't carrying any tools at all. They run out of gas and, because they aren't carrying any charts, they don't know where they are."

And Roger Lancup, a Montreal weatherman, talking about boaters who couldn't read the sky and who hadn't taken a weather course, had this sage bit of advice: "Anybody who does more than dinghy sailing, anybody who plans to be away from his wharf for more than one hour, owes it to himself and to his community to know, when he casts off, whether or not he will be endangering his life or the life of someone else."

THE HOW NOT TO CRUISE GUIDE~~~~~~~~~~~~~

We had reached *that* point in our yearly cruise, the day when we quit speaking to one another and I began to wonder where I could find a bus depot.

As we proceeded into Old Slys lock, just upstream of Smith's Falls on the Rideau waterway, our normally reliable inboard stalled. We didn't need the power to go forward. *Hirondelle* had more than average forward momentum. We needed the reverse to slow down. Jack lunged for the boat hook to grab the nearest vertical rubber-covered chain. He snagged it. The boat hook broke. We managed to shout a warning to the vessels in the lock. There was now a threat of real danger from our 33-foot mast, posed horizontally across our 23-foot wooden sloop like a well-seasoned battering ram. Our potential victims caught us in mid-flight. We survived the lock-through, got the motor running, and tied up on the down-side mooring wall.

Jack stormed directly off to his lonely bunk without eating. Left to bed down the boat alone, I tried to prove something with the bigger toolbox which was nesting over the anti-chafe hose. In slinging it around, I re-injured a back that had gone strange late in June. My spine singing with pain, I organized the boat after a fashion and, totally spent, wandered over to the nearest picnic table and flung myself down.

A car stopped at the crest of the hill overlooking the lock and a young man ambled down to the water. He smiled and continued on to the water's edge, looked around, walked back, turned to me, and said, "Your boat?"

I explained that we were stopping overnight.

"O.K.," he said. "I saw you from the road and you looked like you could use a friend." He strolled back to his car, waved and vanished, leaving me grateful but shaken. If a stranger in a moving car a block away could pick up my mood, there was definitely something wrong with the way we executed our holidays.

We spent the next day recuperating at Smith's Falls. Mostly we found separate corners and spent the day reading. It was night before either of us was in any shape to have a rational discussion.

Even when we were both spitting mad, we knew that there was nobody that either of us would rather be with than one another. However, now we both realized that our last two summer cruises had produced this exact reaction. Given that there was nowhere we would rather be than on the boat, it was a revelation that gave us pause. Genuinely concerned, we decided to give Smith's Falls the benefit of our company for another day while we figured out what was wrong.

Most obviously, we were trying to stretch our holidays too far. This was the second time we had tried to sandwich the Rideau Canal between sailing the Ottawa River and cruising the Thousand Islands and the St. Lawrence Seaway. This year we had been hit by a nasty Ottawa Valley squall. Instead of taking a day to wind down, we had plunged off according to a winter-conceived schedule, blindly putting in the required nautical miles and number of locks per day.

By contrast, I remembered a satisfying trip I had taken with my older daughter, Ruth. We had flown to Calgary and put 2000 miles on our rent-a-wreck with no arguing because we had a few absolute rules. We had no imposed destinations or deadlines so that, although neither of us has any sense of direction at all, we were never lost. You can't be lost when you're not going anywhere in particular.

We also had an ironclad rule that if either of us, for any reason, said, "I want to stop here," we did. We explored every highway marker and road sign, we side-tripped through little towns, we stopped at every duck-encrusted slough, we spent hours at the sides of roads taking photographs.

Now Skipper and I were rushing through the Rideau, by-passing all the interesting gunkholes. I was trying to take photos while taking my turn as helmsman. At the more interesting lock stations, I raced off the boat, snapped a few photos, then leapt aboard as we cast off to continue our relentless trek from buoy to buoy. I love to swim and an allergy to chlorine keeps me out of swimming pools. We never seemed to find time to search out a swimming hole.

The long discussions and the quiet day helped. We consciously tried to slow down. However, it was another couple of seasons before we discovered our real problem. We had fallen into the "Friday Night Departure" syndrome. Jack would race in from work to change clothes while I shut off the typewriter, flinging the last manuscript towards the post office on our way to the yacht club. We would leap aboard and cast off, assuring one another that we'd do the last stowing, fix supper, get organized, and wind down under way. It never happened.

Jack worked for a construction industry sub-contractor with an owner/manager whose management style was most easily described as "crisis intervention." When one project blew up and got too far off schedule, all available resources would be thrown at it, letting other projects slide. Jack was a draftsman and cost estimator. By nature, he liked a quiet and controlled work situation. By holiday time he was too stressed to realize how stressed he was.

I was a child care worker, working front line with emotionally disturbed preteens in a residential treatment centre. My first, mostly unused, training had been in journalism. Some lucky combination of wind, water, boat and fine grade sandpaper had rekindled my creative instincts. I was trying to establish myself as a freelancer around working shifts. I knew I was burned out, but I was too toasted to do anything logical about the problem. We might never have found a fix. Instead, our solution was given to us one summer.

We had planned the usual itinerary. Skipper had booked a month's holiday so we could make for Belleville and the Trent system.

The second day out, Skipper perceived an engine over-heat problem of some significance. We called our friends at Hay Island on Lake St. Francis and Jim towed us in to their dock. For the next three days, Skipper, Harvie and Jim invented remedies and made test runs while I made encouraging noises, drank tea, and did justice to Roz's world famous blueberry muffins.

Still unsure of the results, we gingerly tiptoed westward up through the final St. Lawrence Seaway system lock and crept into Iroquois Marina to get some advice from that area's marine institution, Leroy ("No problem") Hamilton. Leroy's friend, Paul Webb, kept his antique launch, the *Flox*, and her original gasoline engine functioning, so we reckoned that he'd know how to deal with *Hirondelle*'s 40-year-old engine. More tinkering. More test runs. More inconclusive results.

Finally, we decided to venture as far as Brockville where, after a long conversation with the chief engineer from one of the St. Lawrence cruise ships, we accepted the awful truth, the one that had been suggested to us more than once. We had been trying to fix a nonexistent problem.

Between test runs, we had spent a bit of time ambling around the village of Iroquois. As the days drifted by, we began to spend most of our time watching the sweet clover grow. By the time we headed upstream, we were well and truly relaxed and ready to enjoy our holiday. We gave up the idea of Brockville and the Trent waterway and decided to have some fun with our boat.

On a 24-foot wooden sailboat that is expected to carry personal gear for two people, navigation necessities, a typewriter, cameras, reams of paper, notebooks and sharpened pencils, books and Skipper's sketch pads and coloured pencils, we had no room for souvenir buying, except for more books. Therefore, any spare money we had could justifiably be spent on concerts, theatre and eating out, a rare treat after several days of galley cooking. We stopped for every bit of summer theatre we could find along our route, we carefully scouted out the best restaurants, we wandered through old graveyards at dusk when the marble headstones were bathed in the copper glow of the setting sun. Jack took time to sketch old stone and ruins. Rather

46

than detracting from our boating holiday, our new adventures added to it.

We quit snarling at one another. That added an extra measure of pleasure, too.

EXPLORING OUR FAVOURITE LAKE ~~~~~~~~~~

There is only one way to approach Lake St. Francis - slowly, in the evening, coming off the Beauharnois Canal an hour or two before dusk so that all the clichés ever printed can't approximate the sky and the wraparound sunset, backlit by the pastel flashes of the clouds that circle the lake, so that you fire through roll after roll of film, taking the clouds, taking the sunset, taking the bronze glow on your hull as you putter on through the twilight.

Thirty-eight miles long, three to four miles wide, Lake St. Francis begins just past the Valleyfield bridge and fetches up against a cluster of islands nesting east of South Lancaster. Caught between two provinces, it offers bilingual charts, Ontario English names mixing happily with Quebec French, so that it is Lake St. Francis / Lac St-François, and there is Butternut Island and Île Mouton, Ross Island and Île du Grenadier. It was *Hirondelle's* favourite bit of water - given her head, she could probably have found her way to the Beauharnois Seaway locks, up through the Beauharnois canal, and onto the lake all by herself. Fortunately, it was Jack's and my favourite water, too, so we didn't have to argue with *Hirondelle* when she wanted to peel around Ile Perrot to the Seaway.

In the late eighties, the lake was liberally dotted with tiny, free, badly maintained public docks and with bays that offered quiet anchorages in water that was clean enough for swimming. The trick was to arrive at the lee side of the dock first, before any other overnighting traffic, and to keep to the bays in the south side of the lake to find unpolluted swimming water - the other side, according to my local experts, suffering the effects of Cornwall, upstream.

Our Lake St. Francis was Valleyfield, with an attractive park along an historic old canal, and easy access to shopping from the free berth on the old concrete wharf. Parking there required packing along fenders we didn't love overmuch. We'd motor slowly way down into the bay, all the way down, past the marina, past the viewing stands for the July regatta, and we'd make fast, parkside, almost at the main road.

Our Lake St. Francis was the upper end of the old Soulanges Canal, a mooring so pretty it was poetic, with its abandoned lighthouse and weathered footbridges. The canal wall demanded extra long lines and lots of anti-chafe hose, but the walk along the canal bank, with the faint hum of the provincial campground in the background, awarded the little effort. We continued to go back, even after we discovered that this was not the hurricane hole it looked to be - after we experienced, firsthand, a line squall that slipped up the canal, all unannounced.

Our Lake St. Francis was St. Anicet, birthplace of the Léger brothers, Cardinal and Governor-General. It is a little town surrounded on three sides by cornfields and on the fourth by water. The historic park offers commemorative plaques on a grassy area tucked up under the giant willows near the dock, the former Léger house still stands beside the park, there is good swimming at a regulated beach and fine fishing off the dock. The magnificent Byzantine-domed church is as friendly and welcoming as it is imposing and historic, a point of reference for mariners that has graced the lake for more than 100 years.

The St. Lawrence River Pilot (Canadian Edition) Montreal harbour to Kingston harbour and including Ottawa River, Corrected to Jan. 1, 1933, published by Canadian Hydrographic Service, described St. Anicet as "a small village on the southeast shore. Its church is a very ornate and imposing edifice, the dome being particularly conspicuous and serving as a useful steering mark. A depth of 7 feet can be taken to the wharf." Back in 1933, when the defined channel depth was 14 feet, the Pilot book continued, "St-Anicet shoal with 5 feet of water over it lies off Pointe Caissonnettes and St-Anicet, its length northeast and southwest being 2-1/2 miles, separated from the shore bank at those places, by a channel 200 yards broad and 20 feet deep. The Ship channel, a third of a mile wide, with not less that this depth, passes between St-Anicet shoal and Pointe Mouillée flats. On the northwest edge of St-Anicet and on the southeast side of the ship channel, is moored a black cylindrical light-buoy, showing an occulting white light. It bears 352 degrees distant one mile from St-Anicet church. The ruins of a small pier, about 10 feet high, lie close southeast of the buoy on the edge of the bank. The pier originally supported St-Anicet shoal light house, which has disappeared."

Sailing Directions, Great Lakes, Volume 1, Tenth Edition, 1986, has corrected that entry to read: "St-Anicet, pop 245 in 1981. There is an ornate and imposing church with a particularly conspicuous silver dome. At St-Anicet there is a Public Wharf with an outer face 58 feet long and a depth (1983) of 7 feet alongside. The deck of the wharf has an elevation of 4 feet."

No mention of the ruined lighthouse.

But Lake St. Francis is a place of legends proven true.

"McKillop's Light was on a little rocky island," Paul-Emile Cardinal Léger told me during an interview in the mid-eighties. "The keeper was a Scot by the name of McKillop, the typical original man. He never married, but he was a faithful Catholic and every morning after his night in the light he would attend Mass, rowing over in his rowboat at half-past six just so he could assist at Mass, then rowing off to his home. I never knew where it was.

"One day he didn't come back. What happened? We never knew. Everyone searched to find poor McKillop.

"After ten days, a Scot came to us. 'You French Canadians,' he said, 'you don't understand. I will go sprinkle my oatmeal and, like a fish, he will rise to the bait'."

"He did," said the Cardinal. "He came up to smell the oatmeal."

There is absolutely no sign of McKillop's Light or a McKillop's Point on Lake St. Francis charts. But one night on Hay Island, while we were brooding over old charts during a Lake St. Francis gale, we found the old light. McKillop's Point had been renamed Cantagner and that had been changed to Pointe Caissonnettes, the current name.

Oh, but there was magic at St. Anicet. The rough, battered little dock under the willows never disappointed. There was always room for *Hirondelle.* St. Anicet was our storm haven, whether we were running from one of Lake St. Francis' more elegant three-day gales or storms of the soul and spirit. Cardinal Léger had warm memories of growing up there surrounded by "real happiness, security and tolerance," and some of those blessings had been left behind for us.

I'd scamper up to daily Mass, the ritual comfortable even though Mass was in French. Like as not, the late Fr. George Quenneville, another St. Anicet native, would spot me and offer to feed breakfast to Jack and me. Like the Cardinal, he had a soft spot for anyone who loved his town, his lake, and that wonderful old church which was the work of a priest with, he said, "some grandiose ideas." The priest thought that if he built a cathedral, St. Anicet would become the centre of the diocese. His tactic didn't work. The real cathedral is in Valleyfield - but the beautiful old church is a lasting legacy

In some unidentified direction from St. Anicet lies Hay Island, the ultimate Camelot without the sad ending. Hay Island is not really Hay Island, but that tiny paradise is the summer home of D. Harvie and Roz Hay and their son, Jim. Feeling that good friends needed some privacy, I chose to rename their home when side trips there first cropped up in a yachting magazine article.

This was one Lake St. Francis tactic that did work. It also called the wrath of a frustrated boater down upon my head. He had diligently searched the charts looking for the elusive bit of land, planning to make an unannounced visit. I found out when he passed his rage onto the magazine editor who subsequently told me about the phone call.

Hay Island is not a big place as islands go - it holds a cottage, a boathouse, a clothesline, enough lawn for some lawn chairs, a dock, and some beautiful 60-foot trees. It is also home to the most determined beaver in the east. At last count, he had managed to fell one 60 footer and was hard at work on two more. Fortunately he had the foresight not to drop his first booty onto the cottage. How he intends to haul it away is beyond all of us, though, unless he intends to make a raft of the next two trees and float it away. What is a beaver going to do with a 60-foot tree? We can only assume he has heard that the Seaway locks are in poor repair and he intends, as Canada's prime symbol, to restore them to maintain Canada's maritime pride.

Or, maybe he just wants to float them around to dockside. Seems that, every spring, when the ice comes out, it takes chunks of the Hay Island dock with it. Every year, Jim performs the Hay Island ritual rebuilding. The act seems to be his annual rite of passage into summer.

Like many inland sailors around Montreal, we were locked into sailing round and round the "Golden Triangle," Lake St. Louis, Lake of Two Mountains, Ottawa River, Rideau Waterway, Kingston, Thousand Islands, St. Lawrence Seaway and back to Lake St. Louis. We liked the adventure of sharing the Seaway with 730- foot freighters from romantic sounding places. We liked exploring the historical towns along the Rideau. I favoured the swimming in the Thousand Islands and the good summer theatre around Gananoque. We liked the less crowded sailing in the "big water" around Kingston.

But our spiritual home was Lake St. Francis. Several times each summer, the lake would call, and we would have to respond.

Hirondelle at Hay Island

Church at St. Anicet

The Seaway and Beauharnois Canal

A LEARNING WEEKEND ~~~~~~~~~~~~~~~~~~~~

The weather had been hot and airless. Since we weren't accomplishing anything at home, it seemed to make sense to escape onto *Hirondelle* for a long weekend. We decided to pop up to Lake St. Francis and make for Hay Island. While Skipper did boating chores, my portable manual typewriter and I would finish a couple of articles that simply were not writing themselves in the clammy city heat. Between times, we would go sailing. We'd visit with Roz. Skipper would give Harvie a hand with some carpentry. I'd swim or discuss the vagaries of the freelance market with my writing buddy, Jim.

Even though we were hot and anxious to be away, we did all the necessary safety checks: foul-weather gear on board, gas tank filled, engine checks done, boat given a last visual inspection, VHF radio tested, water tanks filled, food and clothes on board. We certified ourselves ready to go.

The weather broke Wednesday night. Thursday was cloudy and windy, but the marine forecast promised better times ahead. Marine forecasts are not always accurate for one's immediate area. Considering that a forecast is often given from Gananoque to Donacona, a precise reading for a particular stretch of river is not always available. I had taken the CPS weather course, and I had a private barometer: violent migraine headaches. I ignored all personal warnings in favour of the forecast. I wanted a holiday.

Even though the big Seaway locks were open for us and we didn't wait at either bridge, we used a third more fuel than usual motoring up the Beauharnois Canal which connects the Seaway portion of Lake St Louis with the Seaway portion of Lake St Francis. In the face of mounting, contrary winds, neither of us was prepared to struggle across Lake St. Francis, so we made for the free public wharf at Valleyfield. It was a wet, rough ride.

Noble to the end, I suggested to Skipper that he tuck himself up with a book and get warm while I got supper.

I knew about hypothermia, in an academic, theoretical way, from our CPS courses. I'd always associated it with freezing into a snow drift or falling into cold water, though, intellectually, I knew that even with dry cold, there was a possibility of some impairment of judgement. However, I wasn't prepared to learn I couldn't work our alcohol stove. I primed it, I lit it, I couldn't stop it from flaring up. Worried that I'd warm up when I set the galley on fire, I finally called Skipper who, warm now and rational, discovered that I was turning the dial to "clean" rather than to "off." I was creating the flares. Skipper took over the galley and I went to bed.

By Friday the weather hadn't improved. We made a slow, rough passage, grateful that there would be hot tea waiting for us at Hay Island. By Saturday, the marine forecast had caught up with my head and with reality. Channel 16 was filled with weather watches and weather warnings for thunderstorms, squalls and gales. Even with *Hirondelle* on the inside of the Hay Island dock, she bucked and bumped.

We had prepared the boat. We had not prepared ourselves. Fortunately, we had each picked up a sweater and a jogging suit, but mostly we had warm-weather clothes. Our foul weather gear would have been useful had we been going anywhere, but, in the face of gale warnings, we simply added another line to *Hirondelle's* defence, and stayed put. It was too rough to type, even in a protected harbour. It was too rough for boating chores. It was too rough to curl up with a book in a bunk that could have used the quilts that we had left at home. It was too wet for me to prowl around with my camera or for Harvie and Skipper to do much serious carpentry.

I realized that, when we had provisioned the boat, we had worked from hot weather menus: lots of salad ingredients, fruit juices and cold cuts. No soups or stews. We were, of course, tucked up beside a fully equipped cottage with a magic tea pot that never ran dry. Our charming hostess just happened to be a gourmet cook. We could hardly say we were in a tough situation. However, had we been anchored out and experiencing near gale force winds, we would have been thoroughly cold and uncomfortable by the time the weather moderated on Monday. It was, in fact, still so rough that we accepted Harvie and Roz's offer of a drive back to the city. It wasn't the first or the last time that Hay Island had extended guest privileges to *Hirondelle*.

I grew up on a farm near Leslie, Saskatchewan. I spent my teen years in Foam Lake, a small town. In winter, no one ever got into a car without shovels, chains, heavy boots, thick socks, a good parka, adequate headgear, candy bars, old newspapers and matches. Packing a survival kit, just in case, was a normal part of preparing the car for winter.

It was time to put some of those prairie winter lessons to practice on the boat. Packing a survival kit became a normal part of readying *Hirondelle* for the summer. We equipped the boat with quick hot-meal ingredients, soups and hot drinks that could be prepared with a minimum of fuss under way, if need be. Cold-weather clothes and quilts went on board in the spring and stayed there all season.

When I had been packing three little kids back and forth across Canada, their activity kit was as essential to my sanity as their changes of clothes. Skipper and I made an activity kit for the boat. It included my weather course notes, for a little refresher.

We had always been careful about tending the boat. In one weekend, we learned that, in the interests of safety as well as comfort, we had to take the time to be careful about preparations for ourselves.

LET'S REMEMBER WHOSE SPACE IT IS ~~~~~~~~~~

We were puttering around the Thousand Islands, looking for a place to drop anchor, swim and have lunch. The couple on the park island waved us towards the last available dock space.

"No thanks," we shouted, "we're just swimming."

They insisted. We changed course and made for the dock.

"Thanks," they said. "We're supposed to meet friends here for supper, and we can't reserve dock space for them. Would you mind staying here until they come?"

We were happy to protect the space for the afternoon. I had my swim, we ate, and we lazed around waiting for their friends. I made some foolish remark about the joy of actually living in the islands.

She gave me a long look. "We natives abandon the islands in May. About corn roast season, we get them back."

Oops.

I thought about the times we had crabbed about the chop from big boats going too fast in narrow waterways, about no docking space, no decent anchoring, overcrowded restaurants, passage complicated by having to dodge sightseeing cruise boats, and big cruisers and sailboats manned by crews who believed they had the right to tack into headwinds in a narrow channel. I wondered how I'd feel if all this were happening on my own doorstep. Two years later, I found out. Our hometown was "discovered."

Ste. Anne de Bellevue is an old French Canadian town at the western tip of Montreal Island, with Lake of Two Mountains on one side, Lake St. Louis on the other, and the Ste. Anne rapids and lock between. It was a boating centre before the Hudson's Bay Company established a trading post for the voyageurs who had to portage around the rapids.

In 1843, part of the rapids was tamed with a canal and a lock to facilitate steamboat and barge passage between the two lakes. In 1978 the lock and surrounding land were taken over by Parks Canada who now maintains it for pleasure craft.

The approach wall to the lock once made a fine place to tie up during our weekend forays from our yacht club to Ste. Anne's for ice cream. Even though our house was only a few blocks from the canal, sometimes we'd overnight there aboard *Hirondelle* to get an early start on our weekend cruising. Sometimes, when I was working shift work and couldn't get away on the weekend, we'd simply sleep along the canal, letting the gentle movement of the water rock us to sleep.

Unfortunately, Ste Anne's was discovered. It was discovered by the owner of one very large cruiser. He would deck himself out like a "real" captain in whites with lots of gold braid and, as he pulled up along the canal wall, would pick up the bull horn. "Hey, there, shift that dinghy. Move that sailboat back. The green runabout is in my way." He wanted - and took - the spot directly alongside the terrace bar. People walking along the canal were often so taken aback by his arrogant commands that they did indeed run about moving other people's boats.

The canal was also discovered by a crowd of weekenders who liked to raft up in rows across the width of the canal, so that passage into and out of the lock was also impossible.

It was discovered by a group of yahoos who liked to whip into the mouth of the canal in the evening, making high-powered, high-speed turns so that they could watch boats bouncing off the canal wall.

Lock at Ste. Anne

One of our little canalside restaurants was discovered by a fellow who stood at the counter, pounding on it with his fists, shouting, "I want service and I want it right now!" We watched visiting yachtsmen fight to be the first into the lock, first out. We listened to them demand fast food service at a restaurant where we locals valued the charm and ease of pace. We wondered why some holidayers were in such an all-fired rush. We speculated that if we spent two weeks in July running over boat owners' shiny white foredecks in muddy work boots, there'd be howls, shouts and lawsuits. Those vacationing boaters weren't treating our little hometown with much more respect.

No, we who own boats don't own the world. The towns and villages along our nation's inland waterways really aren't a collection of marinas run by incompetents. They do not, Brigadoon-fashion, disappear into the mists at the end of boating season, to reappear whole, strictly for our use, at the beginning of the new season. They are, rather, the homes of people who are remarkably like us.

Once we finally learned to slow down and to look around, to accept the notion that a cruise could be more than fanatical plotting on a nautical chart, Skipper and I discovered that, often, the best part of the trip was meeting local people and becoming part of local events.

After all, much as we called our summer vacations a sailing trip, we were also honest enough to admit that we could count on a wind from the east when we were going east and a wind from the west when we were going west. There were also days with no wind and days with blustery winds. There were days when the Thousand Islands were too crowded for a sailor with a conscience to raise a sail. Some holidays were made practically all under sail. Others were made under motor. Until we could control the weather, we couldn't find any other solution.

But there were always people to meet and stories to hear. There were always people willing to help with my search - the day I decided I had to get into St. Mary's church, half the town of Newboro set about locating the minister for me.

It was worth the day. St. Mary's is an historic little church built from stone quarried on a farm on the Little Rideau, then drawn by 40-horse teams to the site. Of Saxon design with high side walls and a square tower surmounted by a belfry, it was old, elegant and beautifully maintained. We took a stroll out of New-

58

boro to the St. Mary's cemetery where we found a monument to John Chaffey of the Chaffey's lock family, and his wife, Mary Ann Tett, whose family had donated the land for the church.

In contrast to the soaring white pillar topped with an acorn, symbol of resurrection, across the street we found the Old Presbyterian cemetery with a stark black-and-white sign acknowledging that the sappers and miners who died of malaria building the waterway were buried here in unmarked graves.

Those unmarked graves for the men who gave their lives for Colonel By's dream of a waterway connecting Ottawa and Kingston bothered us. It didn't seem fair.

On our next Rideau trip, we found their monument in Smith's Falls.

The canal labourers were Irish and French. They worked all day, waist deep in stagnant water. Malaria was common, medical care was non-existent. The nearest hospital in Brockville was inaccessible because of the lack of roads.

In Smith's Falls, in 1829, a group of workers met formally for the first time and by 1832, the year the Rideau was finished, they had a frame Catholic church. Their church is long gone, but in its place is the church of St. Francis de Sales, patron saint of writers and editors, an ornate church with frescoes and carved angels and stained glass windows with two-inch-thick hand-chiseled glass inserts.

In Perth, at sunset, with copper light glinting off the monuments, we prowled an old cemetery across from the public dock, an ancient friendly place full of worn marble slabs. Perth, we discovered from one of the locals over coffee, is the site of the last fatal duel in Canada.

Off Gananoque, we joined the local population in an ecumenical vesper service at Half Moon Bay among the Admiralty Islands. The bay is tiny, with soaring rock walls. The acoustics are miraculous. The congregation worships from their own boats. Boy Scouts in canoes paddle around and hand out hymn books. The atmosphere invites meditation and contemplation. For 100 years, boaters have gathered in the crescent shaped bay tucked into the northeast corner of Bostwick Island. A stone slab serves the presiding clergy, and holds the portable organ. The first time we attended, the organist began to play at 4 p.m., the bay filled with lavish sound, and we knew why people returned again and again.

All we had to do was let someone know we were interested in history, in a scenic walk, in a story of the area. As a writer, I gathered the histories, the scenery, the stories as natural resources. Even when I couldn't sense a possible magazine article, we romped off, collecting memories just for ourselves.

I sometimes wished that some of the boating visitors to Ste. Anne had stopped me on the main street. I'd have sent them for lunch to the Simon Fraser house where, according to local legend, Sir Thomas Moore wrote "The Canadian Boat Song" after he had watched the voyageurs portage around the Ste Anne's rapids. I'd have walked them over to the Hudson Bay House that was eventually remodeled into flats. I'd have suggested they visit our historic French Canadian church, one of the oldest on the Island of Montreal. I'd have directed them out to our beautiful college campus. I'd have been pleased to share our history, our scenery, our stories with visitors.

Rideau Canal

Jack and son John

In the Rideau Canal

VISITORS ~~~~~~~~~~~~~~~~~~~~~~~~~~~~~~~~~~

There was an advantage to the boat over a cottage. It was more difficult for people to drop in on the boat, wondering whether or not we weren't lonely yet, and would we like some company. And we were spared the job of feeding and cleaning up after half a dozen people.

Generally speaking, I like people. I am just not very fond of people who figure that the best way for me to spend my holiday is in catering to them in awkward spaces with limited resources.

I spent one summer at a cottage out of Ottawa, a temporary place while we waited for an out-of-country posting that never did materialize. With two babies in diapers, a wood stove, a back yard pump, a scrub board and lines strung through trees, it was a little closer to pioneer life than I was ready to manage.

I would have loved city friends to arrive every weekend with stacks of pizza boxes and cartons of Chinese food take-out, to scoop up our week's supply of laundry and return the previous week's offering.

Instead, our city friends came out to play at the lake, secure in the knowledge that while they swam, boated and drank, a meal and some tasty snacks were being prepared for them. Sunday night, they would leave for the city, telling us how lucky we were. I'd look at the dishes, wonder whether the local skunk was out by the pump, decide I'd leave all the dishes for Monday, and promise myself only one promise. Never again.

Therefore, no cottage. Therefore, the boat.

We hung around with a barbecue crowd. However, Skipper had none of the typical North American fondness for large hunks of meat. Years of eating lunches in Montreal restaurants had given him a taste for sauces and seasoned foods. He was also passionately fond of rice and pastas in preference to potatoes. We sometimes barbecued with the group, just to be sociable. However, most of the time, there were just the two of us on board, looking for a meal.

The advantage - for an introvert - of sailboat cruising is that sailors are, generally speaking, fairly independent, and rather than insisting on eating "in group" every night, unless we all went out together, we would separate for meals and gather later for coffee.

Hirondelle was really too small for any sane couple to invite people for longer than a weekend. There were tiny bunks forward - just enough headroom to allow for reading in bed or for Jack to sit on his bunk to eat. There was also a tiny bench that was supposed to be another berth but was too short for any human we ever met. The weekend we had Jack's daughter and son-in-law, Janet and Rick, aboard, Janet got the "bit of a bunk" and Rick got the galley floor. Unfortunately, it rained and the hatch leaked. In the morning we discovered a good-natured Rick asleep with a pair of pots on his chest to catch the drips.

Rather than trying to sleep people on board, it was much better sport to invite three or four people to spend a day with us on the water. I'm not totally antisocial though I do have the introvert's need for extra privacy. Skipper would get real pleasure from letting visitors take over the helm. With Skipper crewing, there wasn't much for me to do except pour juice and relax. I rather enjoyed it.

As for feeding company, I've grown older and wiser than during those cottage days in the early sixties - and so have the people around me. My honourary French Canadian son, Marc, announced one Thanksgiving that, henceforth, all festive family meals would be pot luck because Mom was spending too much time in the kitchen. With each family creating one or two of their specialties, our festive meals have become feasts.

As our family grew and matured into their own aims, ideals and attitudes, we developed quite a group of vegetarians. My son, Joe, followed a macrobiotic diet for several years, quitting when, as he told me later, he realized that it made him anti-social. He couldn't eat with his friends, and he couldn't go out to most restaurants. He is a vegetarian although he does eat fish.

Cooking for vegetarians, especially when they also ate fish or dairy products and/or eggs, was an asset on a boat without refrigeration. We didn't have to worry about keeping steaks fresh. The only problem about a mixed feast, in fact, is that the family vegetarians complained bitterly that "the carnivores" were gobbling up their special treats.

There wasn't room in *Hirondelle*'s galley for one person, let alone two. When we had company, Jack and I took turns cooking. Guests were encouraged to feel at home by doing the dishes. Jack and I would take our cups of tea into the cockpit -

the better to stay out of their way - and let our visitors enjoy to the full all the delights of cruising aboard small craft.

We rarely had little people on board. It wasn't a boat rule. There just weren't many children around

Some years ago, before Jack had met either *Hirondelle* or the First Mate and was temporarily between boats and crew, he had been offered the use of a small sailboat. The understanding was that, since the owner was tied up all summer trying to establish a new business, Jack would take the owner's wife along when he used the boat. All was well until she brought along the two preschoolers.

Jack asked her to put life jackets on the kids. She refused. "They'll stay in the cabin," she assured Jack. They didn't.

The wind picked up. Jack discovered that the tough job of tacking back to the yacht club was compounded when there were totally unprotected babies playing on the deck.

He never again took the boat out. "If it had been my boat," he said, "we'd never had left the slip without life jackets on those kids."

Having kids along can make or break a holiday. It's more a case of how much the kids can fit into boating life, its rules and its limitations, than on weather and destination. One of my daughters, back in the days of the black sailing canoe with the pontoons, would greet each sailing venture with tears and pleadings of, "Take me home and baby-sitter me."

Sometimes, there are wonderful surprises.

When a Montreal Optimists' Club ran a safe-boating series for elementary school children, we were talked into offering our boat as part of a day-long outing. One of the children was reported to be a real trouble maker. Because I was a professional child-care worker, he was assigned to our boat, as was another young fellow who, we were assured, was no trouble at all.

The "good" youngster was bored. He wanted to be on one of the speed boats, not our little five-knot wonder, and felt no concern about letting us know. We passed him off to someone else for the return trip.

The "problem" child? He was absolutely fascinated with every aspect of *Hirondelle*. Under Jack's careful guidance, he took the helm for a while and sailed our little boat. He was a delight to have on board, and, at day's end, we were sorry to see him go.

Family picnic: Joan, Jack, Ruth, Raphaël, Lucie, Jim, Inga, Leacy

With Inga and Leacy at Cornwall

Jack, daughter Janet, Rick ⇑
Joe and Jack ⇓   Marc ⇒

66

IT'S SUPPOSED TO BE FUN, ISN'T IT? ~~~~~~~~~

There was, Jack muttered to me, something very strange about this launch. He couldn't figure out exactly what it was. He was simply left standing on the beach feeling vaguely uncomfortable.

I flung myself back into the water and encouraged the *Maria Oddney* to snuggle up against the dock, checking for nails, bolts and other potential hull-grabbers in this, her new home on the little Saskatchewan lake with the luxurious clean water and long sandy beaches.

Storms, Eric reminded me. Can't tie her down too tightly. He knew the lake. In fact, he had arranged for the loan of one side of the dock next door to his cottage for my 21-foot F Class 40-some-year-old planked wooden racer.

I was open to advice. Fishing Lake is shaped like a bowl, a bowl that fairly often has a giant blowing bubbles across the length of it. Coming from Ste. Anne de Bellevue, we were accustomed to yacht clubs with inner harbours, or inlets and bays which could provide adequate protection for a boat. We weren't sure how to dock or moor a boat out in the open.

A couple of posts were needed, and a mallet to pound them in, Eric decided. Someone found posts. Someone else found a mallet. The first post split on the third whack. Someone found another one.

Jack called me again. "I've got it," he said. "It's too quiet."

The last bout of radiation had left Jack a little out of shape for launching boats. It was the first time he had done a launch stranded on shore. The new position gave him a fresh outlook.

I dripped over, considered splashing him so he'd feel like he was part of the action, thought better of it, and asked what he meant by quiet.

"When that first post split," he said. "One of the guys just found another one. No one was screaming."

I stood on the beach and watched.

The fellows were experimenting with various ways of taming the *Maria Oddney*. In fact, they were not yelling at one another.

"Remember the first time?" I asked Jack. We'd brought the *Maria Oddney* down to our yacht club to launch and sink her. I'd bought the boat, an ancient craft built in Montreal as part of a fleet of racers, because I needed to prove I could perform on boats the work that I glibly wrote about in various yachting magazines. Jack was the boat builder but this was my job. He provided the teaching and encouragement when I needed it. I peeled the boat down to bare wood, learned to install cotton caulking, and got the craft into usable shape. The rest of the details, including a couple of soft spots, could wait a year.

We had a little problem with that launch. More than one, in fact.

First problem was the club members who swarmed the boat, shouting to Jack, "Why don't we ... We'll have a good time with ... Let's change...." while Jack patiently chanted his new mantra: "This is Joan's boat. This is not my boat. This is Joan's boat."

Second problem was the fellow who climbed inside, poked around muttering humph, and ohh, and hmmmmm and sadly told me that he "could get her back into shape again, but it was going to cost me $2,000." Given that I hadn't asked him for his advice, his inspection or his help, and considering that *Maria Oddney* had cost $500 with maybe $150 for repairs, I figured he could safely and logically be ignored.

It was tougher to ignore the six skippers who decided to launch the boat. I could tell they were all skippers - they were all giving instructions. There were, also obviously, no crew members around - there was no one following orders.

The Keystone Cops might well have taken six skippers launching a 21-foot wooden sailboat that didn't belong to any of them and which they had never seen before as their basic role models.

No one suggested I might have a right to some decisions about my own boat. I decided that it was going to be more fun watching the comedy than arguing ownership. After all, the cosmetic work wasn't going to be done until the following spring.

Jack was on the mark. This launch was different.

We - Jack, the three cats, the two boats and I - had moved to small town Saskatchewan in 1992. We found our particular Shangri-La in Foam Lake, just 15 minutes from the regional park, Fishing Lake. We had sold our much loved *Hirondelle*. However, the *Maria Oddney* and the 12-foot Teal class sailboat that Jack had built for me seemed perfect for local conditions.

So, we discovered, were the people we met. The fellows on this Saskatchewan beach weren't skippers. They were mostly farmers and teachers. They all had some experience with boats. More importantly, though, they were all committed community volunteers. They had enormous experience with working together, getting things done, finding the most practical solution to a problem, and enjoying the moment. They were having fun. So was I. Even from the beach, Jack was, too.

But, according to many seasoned cruisers, pleasure boating is hell, a struggle against the elements for the most primitive survival. "... worst storm on the lake - waves musta been twelve feet high, but I sailed 'er right out ... spent six hours beating into twenty-knot winds ... thunderstorm ... squall ... gale-force winds ... fog so thick, I couldn't see the compass ... anchor dragging...." Some of these fellows, apparently, haven't had a pleasant cruise in twenty years. Interestingly, but not surprisingly, it seems the degree of danger and the number of life-threatening incidents increases in direct proportion to the number of novice cruisers within earshot.

Man's need to prove himself (never generalize) on the water sometimes takes strange twists. A pair of sailors who were, otherwise, quite decent chaps, met a couple who were highway cruisers tempted to try sailing. The intrepid duo offered to take the couple out for a little taste of the sport. The foursome hit the marina some three hours later, the experts congratulating themselves on a fine bit of sailing.

"Sure showed them a thing or two. Man, we had that sucker over on her ear all the way down the lake - got her windows washed for true. Hey, did you see the way I shaved that last buoy?"

The guests?

She staggered to their trailer, white-faced, in the throes of a violent, stress-induced migraine. Her husband followed her, in absolute silence. They've probably never been near a boat since.

Give Skipper credit. When the first fine flush of excitement wore off, he realized what he had done. The former ski instructor who had introduced me, at 40, to my first pair of ski boots and downhill skis, who had had the presence of mind to hire the most competent instructor he could find, who encouraged and supported me so that, in spite of vertigo and a fear of heights, I learned to love skiing and beat him in a ski week downhill race, this teacher of CPS safety and boating courses, this same man had forgotten all his own principles in a momentary thrill of the kill.

It was a lesson that was more profound because both he and I were migraine victims. He knew first hand the degree of pain caused by his participation in the "joy ride" caper. The memory of this one incident changed his approach to sailing. He became much more sensitive to visitors and to his Crew.

As Skipper's first boyhood boat had been a sailing canoe, when I wanted something of my own as a practice craft, he agreed to build me a double-ender, a Teal class 12-foot modified, to my specification, so that she is cat rigged. The first time I took her out, I misjudged the location of the famous Hay Island rock pile. I was rewarded with a rudder that removed itself entirely from my boat. I learned to sail by first rescuing the rudder, then single-handing back to the Hay Island dock with only a sail to steer by. I loved it.

Skipper and I ultimately agreed. Boating is meant to be enjoyed.

The Dragon Boat

LOOKING BACK ~~~~~~~~~~~~~~~~~~~~~~~~~~~~~

When we made the decision to leave Quebec, we spent months figuring out exactly what we, as a couple, wanted from a new home, what our important needs were, what our most important interests were, how we would integrate as two adults with three cats, two boats, wood-working tools, stained glass equipment and the pile of paraphernalia that travels with a full-time free-lance writer/photographer.

Maybe the years on the boat stood us in good stead, helping us to understand the absolute necessity of knowing where we were going and why.

It's something we never did understand through all those summers aboard *Hirondelle*.

We both worked fairly crazy jobs - different stresses but same end result. By mid July, we would both need a holiday. We just never got around to having a long discussion about what each of us wanted from that holiday.

I was content just to be aboard *Hirondelle*. The combination of wind in my hair, the soft hiss of the water, the gentle rocking at anchor at night, sunsets, a chance to read uninterrupted, an opportunity to spend time alone with my favourite man - that was all I wanted.

Skipper was restless unless he was moving or rebuilding the boat. Some part of his personality meant that the holiday had to be productive - he had to be able to say we'd done so many nautical miles, so many locks. He liked abstract problems - he took navigation through CPS although we were not planning to circumnavigate the globe and were unlikely, aboard *Hirondelle*, to ever get out of the sight of land.

Because we weren't sure what we wanted, we weren't good at cruising in tandem with other couples. It was too easy to fall into a routine of letting someone else make the day's choices although they suited neither of us.

Our best times were when we travelled alone and our finest cruise was up the Rideau early one September. It rained most of the time, there was almost no other boating traffic, we had an opportunity to meet the wonderful Parks staff who run the locks, and we had fun.

In retrospect, I believe our most useful life learning came from summers aboard *Hirondelle*. We learned that, squabble as we did over small things, in an emergency we worked as smoothly together as though we were one mind in two bodies.

We also learned that, in many ways, our differences worked for us. I had an uncanny sense for spotting problems. Solutions were in Skipper's department. He had the inventive mind.

We stumbled into serious trouble only twice.

The first time was our own fault. At the end of a summer's holiday, both of us obsessed with the idea of getting home, we came out of the St Lawrence Seaway Beauharnois locks and looked hungrily at Lake St Louis, knowing that the yacht club was only a few hours away. We also looked up, listened to the thunder, and watched the lightning.

I had taken a CPS weather course the previous winter.

"Shall we go for it?" Skipper asked.

We should have waited an hour. We should have tied up at the pleasure craft dock at the bottom of the locks and made coffee. We didn't. I convinced myself that the storm was going the other way.

It caught us in the Seaway and as visibility closed down to the length of our own craft, we realized that, if there were any freighters out there, we wouldn't see one until we ran into it. Just as disturbing, we weren't entirely sure where we were in relationship to Seaway buoys and a certain rocky shore.

We didn't panic. I grabbed a handful of bungee cords and lashed down the sail cover which was trying very hard to act as a sail. Hanging on for dear life, I took up a position on the bow, as lookout, leaving Skipper to man the helm.

The squall blew through fairly quickly. They usually do. It only feels like an eternity. When visibility returned, we discovered that there were no freighters around but there were several other small craft, including sailboats with broken stays and shrouds. We were unscathed.

We also agreed we'd never second-guess a thunderstorm again, and we didn't. The other close call was not our fault.

We had scooted up the west end of the old Soulanges Canal relatively near Valleyfield off Lake St Francis. We figured that high stone and concrete made a good little hurricane hole and, having made our usual late Friday departure, we were tired. We had lunch and went to sleep.

I don't know what woke me up. I don't know why I knew there was a storm coming. I woke up Skipper, grabbed a foul

72

weather jacket, and looked for extra line to shore up our moorings. Skipper didn't ask questions. He bolted out of bed and we secured a couple of extra lines before we were hit by a squall that came roaring down the mouth of the canal straight at us.

The level of water in the canal had been so low when we moored, it was all I could do to clamber from *Hirondelle*'s cabin over the wall to reach land. Now *Hirondelle* was trying to park on the grass beside the lock wall.

Again, the whole episode lasted no more than ten minutes. At the end, we realized that Skipper had been sitting braced against the mast, in cut-off jeans, bare legs, bare feet, fending *Hirondelle* off a concrete wall. He could have had both his legs broken. He didn't have a scratch. On the boat, on a hot and muggy day, I wasn't much for formal sleep wear. We discovered that I had been racing around the boat wearing not much more than a foul weather jacket.

We lost great slices of *Hirondelle*'s mahogany rub rail, wiped away as if it were butter. *Hirondelle* lost long streaks of paint. We lost the original mooring lines which, even though they had been protected with anti-chafe plastic hose, were chewed to shreds against the wall. Our damage was insignificant, considering that we were tied up near a low footbridge and, had we not awakened when we did, had we been asleep when the squall hit, the consequences could have been downright ugly. Considering the possibilities, we also lost our nerve and made for the Valleyfield marina.

As we motored east, we heard the marine forecast warning, two hours too late. "Small craft warning. Squall. All small craft take immediate precautions."

We coped with the big ones and struggled with the little differences. Skipper liked a quick in-out swim. I took forever to get into the water, then I didn't want to come out. I liked to climb Georgina Island, up to the top where the pitch pines grow, survivors in the face of wind and weather. Skipper was not impressed with the little climb, though he sometimes came along, just to please me, and always enjoyed the view if not the walk. I liked to lounge around with a book. Skipper preferred to visit with other boaters. He was much more patient than I was about sitting in a self-serve laundry. I liked long evening walks. Skipper didn't. We both liked going on explorations to look for ice cream. He liked rum and raisin. I liked buttered almond.

We shared one love - fractious, moody, stormy Lake St. Francis. We felt that we knew every corner of it, in the daylight and in the dark - except for the night when an unusual string of lighted buoys drove us mad until we realized we were seeing car lights along the highway.

It wasn't all idyllic. *Hirondelle* leaked. She leaked around the mast step, which meant she leaked directly onto my bunk. She also leaked at the joint between the deck and the cabin, otherwise known as the edge of my bunk. Besides, in spring and fall, we struggled with condensation. A good rain meant at least one day at the laundry or a day with bedding strung out around the boat, inelegant, but effective.

There were lots of trips up the Seaway that were cold, wet and uncomfortable - not dangerous, which at least produces an adrenaline rush, but just discouraging, which doesn't produce anything except a sneaking urge to snipe at the person closest to you.

There were lots of nights when we discovered we had picked the wrong side of the dock or the wrong bay when the wind came up, and we spent the rest of the night trying to settle *Hirondelle* down.

Still and all, most of us live cooped-up lives, noisy lives filled with phones and rush hours, stressy lives filled with deadlines and impatient bosses or customers or clients. For the two of us, for Skipper and his First Mate, *Hirondelle* was the escape we needed.

The wind, the sun, a freighter passing in the distance, a mug of hot tea, something interesting in progress in the galley, a swimming beach, the prospect of a walk after supper, Skipper working happily over the charts, the two of us doing what we each enjoyed best. With that memory comes the echo of Skipper's favourite line from *Wind in the Willows*, when the Water Rat says, "There's nothing - absolutely nothing - half so worth doing as simply messing about in boats."

PASSAGES ~~~~~~~~~~~~~~~~~~~~~~~~~~~~~~~~~

The Skipper, the Viking and *Hirondelle* spent eleven summers together before Jack and I made our decision to move from Ste. Anne de Bellevue to Foam Lake, Saskatchewan.

When the Viking became Deck Hand and Crew in 1980, a resurgent need to write things down each time she encountered water, wind, electric sanders and paint, resulted in a jumble of entries in Crew's Rough Log. This one is from May 21, 1980:

> Look at my photo. What do you see?
> Not much, I suppose -
> scattered, shapeless clouds, smudge of water,
> a stretch of flat land holding a cluster of small houses
> and one nondescript church spire -
> a photo from anywhere.
>
> Does it conjure up late evening sun glow
> and Helmut's Shark gleaming white in the boatyard,
> or Eric (the Red) Christopher (Columbus) - he's named
> after them both,
> he claims - chiseling plywood off his centreboard?
>
> Can you see rain lashing thin grey wisps at grey waves
> while, almost dry in the weathered grey boathouse
> I hand-sand mahogany?
>
> Can you know, from my photograph
> that when I fold up in the doorway
> clutching my enamel tea mug with paint-stained hands
> I can see Mercier Bridge
> and feel sorry for the commuters going home
> who don't have a boat to paint and to sand and to love?

Words and photos have the same problem. They almost always leave a sense of something still missing.

Maybe some of the best reminders of life aboard a small boat come from the lingering fragrances of a small boat galley - coffee perking in time to rain beating on the cabin roof, the warm smell of hot homemade soup, the subtle blend of melting cheese over scrambled eggs, herbed tomato sauces, curry and cumin drifting into the gentle night air.

Curry and cumin, cheese and scrambled eggs, tomato and basil and oregano - the talented blending of herbs and spices and basic ingredients could almost be a metaphor for life.

Cruising aboard a small boat is not as dangerous as you would believe if you listen overlong to the sailors who sit at the bar describing all boating ventures in terms of knots of wind and degrees of heel. Nor is it as easy as some advertisers would promise. The truth lies somewhere in the middle and part of the truth is the knowledge and the talents and the capability of the captain and the crew.

For the Skipper and the Viking, one on-going problem was storm-induced, stress-induced migraines. They destroyed my sense of balance and made a nightmare of windy passages. In gusty weather, I never ceased to be a white-knuckle sailor though steady high winds on a clear day I could describe as fun.

I learned to endure the white-knuckling, not making much pretense that this was how I would chose to spend the rest of my life, but not complaining. The problem was that, caught in a migraine, my brain had no idea whether or not the boat was skipping along at a pleasant heel or was upside down in the water. There is a medical term which I haven't bothered to learn. I know what it feels like. That's enough. When Skipper finally realized that I was truly powerless over the mixed brain messages, he elected from that time onward, under migraine situations, to take down sails, get the motor running, and let me take the helm because for some strange reason I felt better if I was "in control." We would get us to a sheltered dock where I could try to sleep off the effects.

It meant he gave up some of his most pleasurable sailing. He did it. Often when I think of him, the line that comes to mind is from "When You Are Old." W. B. Yeats understood: "...But one man loved the pilgrim soul in you...."

The eleven years that *Hirondelle,* the Skipper and the Viking shared provided more than the memory of some glorious sailing weather, a few moments of terror, brief, intense boating friendships and some truly great meals. We learned a valuable life lesson - that in a crisis, we could count on one another.

That knowledge carried us through the decision to leave Quebec, the sale of our much-loved 100-year-old house, the sale of *Hirondelle*, a move to small-town Saskatchewan, and the knowledge that Jack had cancer. We fought over the details, but we knew absolutely that, in the big moments, we were a finely tuned team.

That's not a bad lesson to learn.

A writer by nature, with the writer's blessing of being able to step emotionally into time and place, I recorded another moment into Crew's Rough Log during the summer of 1980:

"We tied up at Boulanger Yacht after a good run to Lachine. I wandered out onto the jetty with my favourite flower-painted white enamel mug filled with good hot tea. It was dark. The wind, unusual for Lake St. Louis at night, was still up and blowing strong.

"I was overwhelmed with sadness. The wind seemed to tug long woolen skirts as they swirled around my bare ankles. The fleet was leaving without me and, warming both my hands around my mug, I watched the boats disappear into the shadows across the lake. I stood there for a long time, sensing the wind catching my shawl and the folds of my skirt, filled with longing and loneliness.

"I walked slowly back to *Hirondelle*, vowing that I would never again be left behind."

Nevertheless, I have been.

Filled with too much grief to phone, when Jack died, his son John faxed a message from Ottawa to Foam Lake on October 22, 1995: "... After a week of cold, miserable, unsettled fall weather, the sun came out this morning - a beautiful fall day, that wonderful freshness in the air and a nice, strong, steady wind, perfect for passage-making...."

Berny, who knows how to turn a pressure cooker into a stove-top oven, sent his faxed message from Baie d'Urfé, Quebec: "My salty Captain of the northern plains, who shared my love of sea and boats, only your aging frame let you down. But still, sparkling in spirit and love for life, you take with you all that vitality on a great journey where most of your peers arrive in tatters, heading off in fine spirit, itching for adventure, curious of the unknown, open to every soul that you meet...."

The first time I made curry without him, I wept, and could not eat it, but the lingering fragrance of curry and cumin and coriander in my Foam Lake kitchen was a benediction and a blessing.

Last summer, visiting daughter Inga and her husband Leacy, I rediscovered the joy of being on the Ottawa River, this time in Leacy's ocean-going red kayak, following Inga in her yellow model, my teacher and guide.

We paddled to the local provincial park for a picnic lunch. Food devoured at water's edge by two hungry people, I discovered, was still a pleasure. The scramble back to the boats and our rapid return to Pointe Fortune in advance of a thunderstorm was an adventure backed up by a solid built-in safety plan.

At home, my little dragon-prowed boat begs for sails, wants me to come out and play, begs to be turned loose on Fishing Lake, fifteen minutes from my house.

For those of us who try to maintain a sparkling spirit and a love for life, there will always be fresh passages.

All we can ask, in our hopes and our prayers, for ourselves and for one another, are fair winds.

SMOOTH SAILING ~~~~~~~~~~~~~~

"My mom reused and recycled, but I grew up feeling there was a never-ending supply of stuff that I could buy, use and toss. I never thought about garbage or using up all our resources." The speaker was an educated, caring, aware person discussing the formation of Foam Lake's volunteer recycling committee.

My mom had survived the Great Depression on a Saskatchewan farm. She never lost the fine art of conserving. Somewhere in a Montreal-area suburb, in the sixties, I, too, fell prey to the television promise of newer, better, quicker, more modern - or as a young friend said recently, when her mom and I volunteered to share the cost of a diaper service for her, "But I can't use cloth. It takes me thirty seconds longer to put a cloth diaper on the baby than to put on a disposable one."

There was no place on *Hirondelle* for conspicuous consumption. There was no place for anything that wasn't essential. *Hirondelle*'s tiny cabin also took me away from chemical cleaners and back to Mom's baking soda and vinegar and borax. It was not easy to air away chemical odours. Baking soda, vinegar and lemon juice were nose-friendly.

The environmental lessons have remained with me.

On the other hand, I did not translate my "tidy boat self" to my "home self," as anyone who has ever been in my office during a writing binge can verify.

Spending every free moment every summer on the boat meant learning, adapting, trying, failing, trying again.

My rule was to try never to make the same mistake twice. That left ample room for new ones.

STARTING WITH THE POTS AND PANS ~~~~~~~~~

My very prejudiced notion is that any boat with a cabin and a galley, no matter how tiny, should also have a permanent supply of pots and pans, dishes and utensils, and storage containers. Even a little boat without a galley should own its own equipment that can be stored somewhere handy. There is no enjoyment, in my very prejudiced notion, in lugging equipment on and off a boat for every trip. Enough to do it spring and fall.

If money is a problem, then a trip or two to a local garage sale should provide all the necessaries for very little cash. You really don't want the Royal Albert on the boat, anyway.

Here are some random ideas that worked for us:

- A three-litre (three quart) saucepan or metal pail with handle and lid, worked for bailing, scooping up wash water, for doing laundry, and for cooking pastas and soup (not simultaneously).
- Two double boilers provided four pots that were accommodating enough to stack.
- On board, I liked both non-stick frying pans and my old cast iron, even though it rusted every so often and had to be re-seasoned.
- Because "instant" was not a choice of ours, we carried a little metal coffee perk, a giant painted enamel tea pot, a tea strainer, and a tea ball.
- We always carried at least two good paring knives and two chopping knives, making our choices so that the knives were just long enough to fit safely into a drawer. (Knives drifting loose around our galley in a blow were not welcome items.)
- I always tucked in extra wooden spoons. They cracked, split, and fell overboard. Handle length was governed by available storage space.
- I passed on the hand mixer. When it comes to beating, blending and whisking, I do really well with a fork and a small bowl.
- Can openers - we always had two. The rule was that one a season quit on us. They probably rusted. We also carried two punch type openers for evaporated milk cans.

- Vegetable tongs doubled as salad server, pasta tongs and meat turner.
- My china rule: one each for each person on board, plus enough for occasional guests. Plate, salad/soup/dessert bowl, mug, glass. It was all Duralex. I don't like eating from soft plastic. For comfort, especially in rough weather, Skipper and I each had a deep-sided Duralex pie plate rather than a conventional dinner plate.
- Cutlery was cheap replaceable stainless. We also carried - and used - chopsticks.
- Mixing bowls - stainless steel, plastic or Duralex - doubled as serving bowls.
- Storage containers - I must confess I saved lidded plastic ice cream containers, yogurt pots and margarine tubs - not terribly stylish but they were durable and the price was right.
- Glass storage jars - for cornstarch, flour, etc. I saved up a batch of jam, pickle and coffee jars. The trick was to find the type of jar that most exactly fit our particular storage space.
- Salt shakers which would keep at least some of the moisture out of the salt were the big challenge, even with dry rice mixed with the salt. The Tupperware four-ounce with the snap-on top kept us in free-running salt for an entire boating season. (On a damp wooden boat, that's a miracle.)
- Skipper was a real fan of freshly ground black pepper. We carried a little wooden pepper mill and peppercorns.
- A good Thermos bottle or two - an absolute necessity.
- Paper towels. Of all disposable products, I would have found my yearly miles of paper towelling the most difficult to relinquish while remaining a happy boater. I used paper towels for washing, wiping, draining, sponging, for hands and for dishes, to clean grease from pots, to scrub out our bilge, and as sturdy paper table napkins. I'm a dedicated reduce/reuse/recycler, but for greasy jobs on our little boat, I always felt it was safer to use paper and get rid of it (in authorized garbage cans - not overboard). We didn't have enough hot water to properly wash scrub cloths and I had no intention of giving up a peaceful, pretty anchorage to find a laundry.
- My preference was a wooden cutting board that could be scrubbed and disinfected

- I carried stacking plastic measuring cups and measuring spoons, the old-fashioned cup and teaspoon variety, aboard *Hirondelle*. However, anyone who believes that my system of recipe development is an exact science and that I did much serious measuring in *Hirondelle's* galley has probably never tried to make supper in a kitchen that insists on bobbing up and down and sideways.
- In tight quarters, safety was paramount. We carried both oven mitts and pot holders.
- Non-rusting scrubbers doubled for cleaning dishes and for scrubbing vegetables.
- The galley also contained waterproof markers, one wide roll of masking tape and a bag of clothes pins.
- A Tupperware plastic pastry sheet created an instant portable table surface that was easily cleaned.

PROVISIONING ~~~~~~~~~~~~~~~~~~~~~~~~~~~~~~~

Our boating grocery lists were very different from our home shopping lists. For starters, the only time we bought meat on a boating trip was when we intended to head directly to the boat and cook it. On the other hand, while we were generally "from scratch" cooks at home, we were enthusiastic on board about our canned potatoes, clams, shrimp, and peaches. We also cheerfully bought biscuit and pancake mix, playing around with additions to the basic mix until we found a taste we fancied.

Three of my most profound migraine triggers are MSG, dark chocolate and large quantities of garlic. We eliminated all three items from our provisions list except for Skipper's own personal stash of garlic flakes.

In 1985, Skipper was invited on a "dream trip" boat delivery to Florida. For several reasons, most of them because the boats were not designed for offshore use, the trip was more nightmare than dream. The leader of the expedition, an otherwise charming and reasonable individual, believed firmly that multinational corporations knew exactly how to proportion the ingredients in a mix to satisfy all tastes, and would not add so much as a sprig of parsley or a whiff of oregano. Skipper spent a month eating the most boring on-board food he'd ever been offered. The experience made him even more adventuresome during his turns in the galley.

Provisioning for *Hirondelle* broke down into three categories: non-perishable staples, long-term-storage fresh produce, and the real perishables - fresh meat, fragile fruits, most breads.

Quantities depended, obviously, on available space and the usual number of people on board. After years of cooking for my kids and all their friends, I over-stocked all the time. Now my greatest feat was to train myself to buy and to cook in reasonable quantities. I would provision the boat in the spring as though on our first weekend out, we were going to be blown onto a deserted island with no fish, fowl, fruit, or water.

My main objective was to learn which foods provided us with the greatest versatility, keeping in mind not only our food preferences but which meals Skipper preferred to cook and which menus were mine. We ran an equal-opportunity galley.

I always tried to remember that the less time we spent in the galley, the more time we had for essential chores - reading, swimming, sunning, sailing, visiting other boaters, or just holding hands, drinking tea and watching sunsets together.

Generally speaking, I discovered I would much rather sail, laze around the deck or read than spend hours below decks preparing meals. However, both Skipper and I enjoyed good food and spur-of-the-moment entertainment.

I remembered the season at our rented cottage where I learned I could not prevent my city friends from coming out every weekend to "keep me company," a euphemism for watching me cook and do dishes while they loafed in the sunshine. The boat was harder to reach, but some of my galley quick tricks trace their roots to that cottage.

In truth, I realize any of these ideas would work for a camping trip or at a cottage. It might even be easier, I suppose, if you weren't working in a kitchen that was 4 foot 8 inches high, 6 feet long and 4 feet wide.

- I never, never brought plastic-encased food on board. Out of the fridge, fruits and vegetables in plastic sweat and rot. I used brown paper bags.

- I swung all the fresh produce in a cotton mesh hammock. First, I took time to wipe all the produce perfectly dry, using paper towels.
- Cabbage, carrots, turnips, lettuce and zucchini like to sail. Onions are temperamental. Fresh spinach should stay at home with the green peppers and cucumbers. Radishes sometimes keep. Sometimes they suck themselves dry from the inside out and collapse.
- We always carried dried green and red pepper, onion flakes and mixed vegetable flakes. We carried dozens of herbs and spices, happy and dry in the waterproof plastic canisters from 35 mm film, labeled with felt marker.
- Apples, oranges, dates, raisins, Greek figs, plums and nectarines keep well. Soft-skinned fruit doesn't. Grapes attract fruit flies. I didn't like sharing a small boat cabin with fruit flies so we lived without grapes.
- Evaporated milk stays fresh for several days out of a fridge on a boat. We did not carry mayonnaise.
- Crackers always lost their crisp so we bought for flavour instead.
- We liked tea, iced tea and herbal teas. We bought good leaf tea in little metal boxes.
- Walnuts go rancid. We stuck to pecans and cashews.
- Cheese in foil and waxed Dutch Gouda kept well on board. We also loved a sharp cheddar called Imperial, packed in a red cardboard box.
- Margarine in plastic tubs kept better than butter.
- Canned baby clams and tins of shrimp for quick company hors d'oeuvres or an interesting snack for Skipper and First Mate were an absolute necessity, not a luxury.
- Also on our necessaries list - fresh parsley, fresh mint for drinks, fresh ginger root and cinnamon sticks.
- Canned pineapple is a natural sweetener. It also puts some excitement back into limp cabbage, when it is transformed into a cabbage/pineapple salad finished off with some freshly ground black pepper and a dash of salt.
- Open applesauce doesn't keep well. The regular cans are too big. I bought baby food jars of applesauce, one-meal size.

- Canned potatoes make the best pan-fried potatoes in the whole entire world. They're also great for impulsive potato salad. They fit nicely into a made-from-cans stew. I wouldn't travel without them.
- Canned mandarin orange slices offer a pleasant lift to salad made from vegetables that aren't quite as crisp as they might be.
- Canned peaches in their own juices are the easiest comfort food on earth, especially as dessert after a bowl of macaroni and cheese.
- Given the balky nature of my alcohol stove, which provided three heats, hot, sputter and off, I stuck to long grain rice. It's much more forgiving. Short grain goes gluey.
- Our spices and herbs were worth every inch of space they took. My little spice containers had two galley drawers reserved for them.
- Each year I discovered another spice without which I could not travel. As out of date and stale as some of my kitchen spices become in spite of my conviction that I will check and replace them regularly, our boating spices and herbs were always fresh. At the end of each season, I took them all home and either used them or dumped them. Each spring, they were all replaced. Maybe that's why our on-board meals tasted so good.
- I was always short of fresh water. Noodles need less rinsing than spaghetti and we discovered that spinach and soya pastas weren't as starchy as the regular type. Besides, they tasted better. Chinese Long Life noodles are a super, non-starchy spaghetti substitute. The variety macaronis are less pasty than the usual refined wheat product. There are steam-fried noodles which are ready in three minutes and need no rinsing. They are good with spaghetti sauce, cheese or butter. They come in a 14 oz (397 g) package.

LONG-TERM STORAGE WITHOUT REFRIGERATION

My ancestors have ranged the seas in open boats since the early mists of time. Keeping foodstuffs safe was of absolute importance to them. Drake's forces may have been able to beat off the Spanish Armada on a diet of weeviled biscuit, dried fish and sour ale, but that sort of fare would never have kept a Viking fueled for the easiest weekend's pillaging, plundering, colonizing or whatever. Jack had a friend who secured some Texas longhorn steer horns which soon adorned an almost-authentic ceremonial horned helmet, which they then ceremoniously presented to me. Jack often suggested that I am a Viking throwback. Certainly, as I conducted my rites of springtime passage by bashing my skull on all available bulkheads and hatches, I realized why Leif and Eric wore helmets - and why their boats had no lids.

The traditional genetic talent necessary for providing and storing food for long voyages into unknown climates was adapted by my ancestors who homesteaded the prairies and stayed to farm. I carried this legacy full circle back to the sea.

Just because some foodstuffs won't keep forever does not mean that I learned to live without them on the boat. I simply learned - at least some of the time - to remember to eat them up before they went off.

There is a difference, by the way, between foods that need special care and stuff that goes onto the boat only if it's going to be used that day or within the hour.

- Bread - it seems to me that hard black breads keep better than white. Or, maybe I just like them better. We discovered that pita bread kept just as well. Of course, we both liked pita, too.
- Tender fruits - handle these as little as possible, wrap them in paper towels to cut down on bruising, watch them for any sign of mould or rotting and remember that my all-time most popular stewed fruit recipe happened because I discovered a batch of dying fruit.
- Jams, jellies and relishes need to be watched for mould. If you make your own, pack some in baby food jars or any other convenient small glass bottles that will fit inside a drawer or a cupboard.

86

- Maple syrup will mould and needs watching. On the other hand, corn syrup is long lasting, and you can't hurt honey.
- Ketchup, opened, will keep, in spite of the "must be refrigerated" warning on the label. It will go off eventually, but your nose will know.
- Chutney - I never refrigerate it, even at home.
- Soya sauce - unfortunately, the commercial stuff keeps better opened and unrefrigerated than the natural, no-chemicals variety.
- Spinach - I adore spinach salad with mandarin oranges, almonds and bacon bits. Every time I take spinach on board and try to keep it longer than a few hours, it turns into wet green mush.
- Peaches bruise and mould before your very eyes. Nectarines last much better. Besides, canned peaches in sweet rich juice make a great snack.
- Fresh mushrooms have a predilection for turning themselves into slimy grey mush.
- Corn on the cob is great stuff if you can get ashore to husk it. Otherwise, every fine little bit of silk will vanish into the bilge and will surface in congregation with other bits of silk, jamming up the bilge pump.
- Leave your plastic wrap at home. Don't ever, ever, ever try to store anything fresh in plastic wrap. Bring fruits and vegetables on board in boxes or brown bags, not in plastic bags. Outside of a fridge, plastic-bagged produce sweats, then rots, then contaminates anything with which it has contact - within minutes, it seems. Plastic around dried noodles is fine, and does keep out the rainwater. Plastic on cabbage produces a sour, sodden mess. Around turnips, it offers nice chunks of mould. Carrots develop running sores within two days. Plums rot from the inside out, so you don't sense trouble until you bite in...
- It bears repeating. If you don't have a fridge aboard, the very fragile produce should have its own hammock that you remember to check at least once a day.

SAFETY AFLOAT ~~~~~~~~~~~~~~~~~~~~~~~~~~~~~~

Probably the most useful items that we carried aboard *Hirondelle* were our St. John Ambulance First Aid Certificates, our matching pair of VHF Marine Radio Licenses and our Canadian Power and Sail Squadrons certificates that attested to the fact that, between us, we had passed basic boating, advanced piloting, navigation, seamanship (sail and power), marine maintenance, marine electronics, and weather.

Hirondelle being a fairly compact craft, she carried a very small crew. I doubled as Head Chef, Weather Officer, Ship's Doctor, Ship's Writer, First Mate and Cabin Girl. Skipper's major responsibilities included Captain, Ship's Carpenter, Sail Maker and Chief Engineer. We shared the duties of Watchman, Navigator, Helmsman, and Sous-Chef. When I first began to travel aboard *Hirondelle*, I was quite content to do cosmetic chores - I learned to wield a mean scraper and paint brush - and to putter around the galley, surfacing occasionally to tug on a jib sheet.

When it became apparent, eventually, that the threesome of the Skipper, *Hirondelle* and the Viking First Mate were destined to become as permanent a combination as anything can be said to be in our transient world, we began to consider longer voyages and to seriously discuss long-term cruising. We read nothing but boating books. Obviously, I needed some CPS courses.

I have never ascribed to the "It Won't Happen To Me" school of philosophy, which is just as well, because it usually does. I was not a competent sailor, but I became the finest crew I could be. By the time I teamed up with Jack, he had been sailing for fifty years. However, I reckoned that should he fall overboard, or get smacked with a vagrant boom, or just develop flu, I would be as alone three miles from shore as I would be 300 miles out to sea. I suspected that my capacity to effect a rescue or bring the boat home safely would depend on more than my ability to season an omelet.

Skipper, who had cut his milk teeth on the gunwales of a sailboat, and who sailed - and restored - a progressive series of fine craft, insisted (overlooking his years of apprenticeship in small day sailers). that I could learn to sail *Hirondelle* as easily as he could. As a little aside, my fairly unscientific polls have shown that this seems to be a common complaint among cruising couples I know. The other side of the coin, of course, is the spouse who doesn't realize that climbing out of the galley long enough to learn how to handle the boat could be a simple life-and-death matter some day.

Skipper attempted to make amends one summer. He brought home a high performance little fibreglass racing machine that was to be my training vehicle.

I went out with him a few times, and I did take the helm occasionally, but I had no urge to take the boat out on my own. Since I would flee to *Hirondelle* just to be on her when the vagaries of onshore living got me down, I was confused until I realized an elementary fact. Plastic boats don't have any soul. Skipper eventually built me my own 12-foot Teal with a genuine hand-carved mahogany dragon on the prow.

While I was waiting for my own boat, I concentrated on becoming safety-wise in and out of the galley.

I took the weather course after a cozy haven, chosen strictly on the strength of a favourable weather forecast, proved to be a sleepless anchorage when local conditions proved to be entirely contrary to the general forecast. I decided I could do just as well at local forecasting. I can.

One of our instructors, a chief meteorologist, asserted that no one can predict accurately for longer than three hours, and that prediction rests on the basis of local conditions. I have become modestly proficient at three-hour forecasting, training that is augmented by migraine headaches that are triggered by approaching changes in weather. Skipper was the Ship's Carpenter. I had a specific inspection duty. Although I am technically challenged, I developed some strange sixth sense that would ferret out problems which Skipper could then fix - he had an instinctive ability to deal with rigging and engine problems, often while we were under way.

I would do a daily visual check on standing rigging, lines, fire extinguisher pressure. On a couple of occasions, we averted serious problems because Skipper was alerted to a loosened cotter pin or floorboards that were about to float loose because the bilge pump had developed indigestion.

We developed our own favourite safety rules around the use of our stove and open flame in general.

- Check stove connections for leaks by smearing dish detergent around the joints. Bubbles are a sign of leaks.
- As soon as you finish using the stove, release the pressure. With propane, shut off the valves. If you don't release pressure, accidentally bumping the controls will spill fuel all over the place. (Yes, I learned that one when I scraped the control handle of our alcohol stove with my head while I was attempting to paint the aft food locker.)
- Keep flammable materials, including galley curtains, away from the stove.
- Keep the entire stove area clean. Wipe up grease spills immediately. Keep the fuel cups clean to discourage flare-up.
- If your stove has a lid, don't close it up until the unit has cooled down.
- NEVER, NEVER, NEVER leave a lighted stove unattended.
- Keep a box of baking soda within easy reach of your stove. It's an almost universal fire extinguisher.
- Don't try to smother a fire with flour. It explodes.
- Don't try to move a grease fire. Smother it on the spot with a lid, or baking soda, or use a fire extinguisher.
- DO NOT use water on a gas or kerosene or grease fire. You'll spread it.
- Don't position your fire extinguisher over the galley stove. In an emergency, you won't be able to reach it.
- If you use your extinguisher, point it at the BASE of the fire, and discharge it completely in smooth, slow, even sweeps, not in quick, jerky bursts that will fan the flames.
- Once you have discharged your fire extinguisher, don't forget to have it recharged at the first available opportunity.
- Remember that Canadian and American regulations forbid the use of stoves or open flames while in locks.
- Use barbecues ashore or mounted over the stern pulpit. If you are cooking in the cockpit, a vagrant wind could toss burning coals around.
- Use solid fuel starter for the barbecue. Don't use gas on board.

- Don't try to save coals for another meal. Dump them overboard. Charcoal is a natural filter. It won't pollute.
- NEVER, NEVER, NEVER use a barbecue in the cabin. In an unventilated space, charcoal fumes are toxic. In simple terms, you can die.
- Plan a fire procedure. Read the directions on your fire extinguisher and know how it operates. Discharge one on a practice run. Don't forget to have it recharged.

There is also the issue of first aid - given that small boats are really a floating collection of knobs, sharp corners, abrasive wires, toe grabbers and projecting metal, anxious to scoop bits out of exposed human flesh. Besides, there are also unexpected hazards. Our old boat seemed to have an affinity for some of them.

We were happily roaring up the Ottawa River one glorious June afternoon, on a marvellous broad reach when, all unannounced, the connection from the main sheet to the boom parted. The boom flew free, then began to beat itself and the sail to death. Skipper got the motor running and the boat headed up into the wind while I clawed down the sails. Once everything was safely stowed and Skipper was organizing repairs, I realized that my thumb felt as though it had been rammed halfway up my wrist. I wasn't sure whether it was strained, sprained or broken. I did know that it hurt. I also knew I wanted to get it strapped down and my arm in a sling.

Skipper had outfitted *Hirondelle* with a proper Marine First Aid Kit. We had kept it carefully sealed in its original plastic wrap to insure sterility.

Skipper fetched the kit for me, and tore it open. We were greeted with pain killers, anti-nausea pills, three tubes of unguents and ointments, some Band-Aids, a bit of gauze, and two feet of adhesive tape. There were no triangular bandages nor was there anything we could use to fashion a split or a sling.

Skipper immobilized my thumb with strips torn from a tea towel and created a sling from old mooring lines. We motored off to the nearest marina.

We threw out the first aid kit and replaced it with one of our own devising. The moral of the story is this: Before you are faced with a medical emergency, know your first aid capacities. Don't trust packaging. Make your own kit. Ask your doctor for advice or consult your pharmacist, a nurse, or your local St. John Ambulance centre. While you are at the St. John Ambulance centre, take their first aid course. Carry the manual on board.

Carry broad-brimmed cotton hats with some sort of fastening so that they won't blow away, and invest in adequate sun block.

When we first went cruising, the idea was to get away from routine, schedule, crowds, newspapers, and clothes. We figured we could cut down on the time we had to spend at laundries by achieving a sort of minimalist wardrobe. Suntans were in, although we were as careful as we could be about avoiding sunburn.

Within a few years, we realized that the sun was no longer our friend. It didn't caress skin. It fried it. Sun, bouncing off the water, off the white deck of a small craft, looked for bare flesh and became the enemy.

We discovered sun screen and Indian cotton. We discovered that if we pinned a length of line to our cotton sun hats and pinned the other end to our sun shirts, our hats could blow off but not away.

We learned to consume more fluids to avoid dehydration, especially when we were on the move under motor without much breeze on a hot and sunny day.

We learned to watch each other for signs of too much sun, figuring precaution was half the solution.

Precaution also became our solution to accidents in the cabin.

We never worried too much at home, beyond spotting one another on ladders in awkward places. However, on the boat, with no neighbour, doctor, ambulance, or handy hospital we became much more careful.

These were some of our personal precautions:

- All pot handles were directed towards the back of the stove, not over the edge where Cook could catch them with an ill-placed arm or hand.

- We wiped up spills immediately. I managed so many cracks on my head from walking into bulkheads that I was not interested in taking chances on slipping on grease.
- Ditto plastic bags. After one rapid trip across the galley and into our sleeping area, I became very careful about the location of the garbage bag.
- We used pot holders and oven mitts all the time. Besides the obvious burn factor, they provided grip in a moving kitchen.
- We tried to avoid leaving knives drifting around the galley. Although I am not tidy by nature, I did learn to stow the knives immediately after use.
- The sink became the best and fastest stowage space when the weather got rough.
- I did not cook when the weather was really awful. My attitude was that the Ship's Cook was on holiday. Trying to juggle pots and boiling liquids while the floor was coming up to meet me was not my idea of fun.

Fire, scalds, burns, scrapes and bruises. All of this, I suppose, can sound fairly terrifying, especially if you are not one hundred per cent convinced you want to go dashing around with just a thin layer of wood or fiberglass between you and an awful lot of water.

However, on one of those perfect summer's evenings, when God has painted a sky full of sunset just for you, and just a lingering hint of curry teases around the cockpit, and you reach for a heavy sweater so that you can sit in the cockpit and watch the stars switch on, one by one ... you'll know ... oh, yes, you'll know....

Rideau Canal

Maria Oddney

Hirondelle

KEEPING IT GREEN~~~~~~~~~~~~~~~~~~~~~~~~~~~~

A serious allergy to chlorine keeps me out of swimming pools. My introduction to a watery life was as a toddler playing in puddles I discovered after rain on the farm. Swimming is the one athletic activity I completely enjoy. A pair of years at summer camp, while fraught with all the normal teenage angst, did provide me with some fine swimming instruction.

Part of life on the boat, and part of visiting Hay Island, included working my way slowly and painfully into the water, inch by shivering inch, then remaining in my aquatic home, as happy as a fish, for the next hour.

I needed clean water.

Maybe that's why I concentrated on being as "green" a boater as I could. Or maybe, I just don't like using chemicals because of my migraine head. Or, maybe, I am simply following in the footsteps of my mother, she who reduced, reused and recycled long before the words became a popular slogan.

The more summers that Jack and I spent on the boat, the more concerned we both became about keeping our environment as non-toxic as we could manage. By the last couple of years, that determination included the drastic decision to skip the anti-fouling. As part of my swim, I was content to work my way around *Hirondelle* with a scrub brush and a cloth, cleaning off nasty green bits. Of course, given that our top speed was about six or seven knots, being slowed down a little didn't make much difference. When Jack wanted to race, he found a friend with a fast fibreglass boat. Anti-fouling *Hirondelle* was not going to turn her into a slick speed machine.

Leaning on my mother's tried and true cleansers, I tried to keep up the boat without chemicals. Most of these ideas I learned from my mother:

- for cleaning the stove, the sink, and all other stainless steel surfaces - a sprinkle of baking soda and a wipe-down with a damp cloth. Baking soda is a scouring power that won't scratch.
- for reducing that damp feeling - bags of silica gel popped into all drawers.
- for bleaching - either borax or hydrogen peroxide

- for cleaning brass - make a paste of vinegar, salt and water in equal parts, leave for 10 minutes, then polish with a soft cloth.
- to clean and sweeten your cooler - sprinkle with baking soda, wipe down with a damp cloth.
- to keep the cooler fresh when not in use - open a package of ground coffee and leave it in the cooler.
- to clean the head - add baking soda. Scrub.
- for washing portholes - wash with vinegar and warm water and polish with a soft cloth or crumpled newspapers.
- getting rid of mildew and mould - wash down with vinegar or lemon juice.
- freshening the cabin air - simmer a little lemon juice in water or save and dry your orange peels and simmer them with a sprinkle of cinnamon or a few cloves.
- don't feel guilty about using J cloth or some version of the product. Just wash them rather than throwing them away after a few uses. They wash and dry really quickly and they last for an amazingly long time.

Carry your own cloth bags rather than accept piles of plastic. Or, cut plastic grocery bags into one inch strips, haul out your # 7 or # 8 knitting needles, cast on 40 stitches, and, knitting each row, knit yourself a plastic shopping bag that is tough enough to carry two cans of paint and, if it isn't exposed to heat, will last 10,000 years. Don't get fancy. Tie knots as you connect one strip to another. Sew up the sides using fishing line nylon, or strips of plastic bag or yarn. Knit handles by casting on eight stitches and knitting to the length you find useful, remembering that the handles will stretch. One plastic grocery bag knits up into about an inch of your carry-all. You are aiming to produce a rectangle that is as wide as you want your bag to be and twice as long. Once you become accustomed to the feel of the plastic "yarn," it knits up quickly. The end product is attractive and a guaranteed conversation starter. Consider casting on and casting off with needles that are one size larger than you use for the body of the bag.

- Speaking of plastic, try to avoid carrying six-packs with those six rings that get stuck over the head and around the neck of curious birds. If you do carry them, take time to snip each ring open before you dispose of it in the garbage.
- Recycle where you can. Tin cans compact if you cut out both the top and the bottom, lay them inside the remaining cylinder, and stomp it all flat.
- Don't discharge your oily bilge water directly into the river. Sop up the yuck with unbleached paper towels and dispose of them carefully.
- Dispose of plastic bags very carefully. Geese eat them, then starve to death because after eating the plastic they can't digest anything.
- Don't snarl, "What slobs. What a mess." Take five minutes and clean up the beach or the camp site. (You'll feel so noble that it will be worth the effort, and it's better than cutting your foot on some jerk's discarded bottle cap.)

Skipper was so involved one day in fibreglassing an aft hatch cover that it was too late by the time he realized his favourite jeans had soaked up so much polyester resin they were stiff. With nothing to lose, he secured a line to his jeans, threw them overboard and towed them, at slow speeds, for two days. The jeans came through the exercise clean, soft and intact and Skipper wore them with double the pleasure for the rescue.

RED RIGHT RETURNING ~~~~~~~~~~

When I first signed aboard *Hirondelle* as First Mate, Cabin Girl and Chief Cook, I had no experience with producing meals from a moving kitchen. My earlier sailing experience had all been aboard day sailers. To compound the problem, my most current cooking was at home where, in a house filled with teens who often brought their friends home for meals, fourteen at table was not unusual. My hundred-year-old French Canadian kitchen accommodated cooking and serving with no undue hardship.

Hirondelle's tiny galley was another situation entirely. So was learning to cook for a crew of two, Skipper and First Mate.

An avid reader who believes the right book can solve all the problems of the universe, I tried to find a truly useful cookbook.

The first ones offered up shipboard menu after shipboard menu, all of which required at least one item flambé. Flambéed anything in *Hirondelle*'s galley would have set the cabin roof on fire. The next lot of cookbooks assumed blenders, mixers and a good conventional oven. We were a little short on all counts. The third attempt turned up on-board cookbooks that relied on fresh lobster, fresh crab and oysters on the half shell. We were floating around the Seaway system. According to one American study of the time, eating one large Lake Michigan trout would exceed the government's norms for a lifetime's acceptable cancer risk. Zebra mussels had become plentiful, but were a little small. Neither of us liked fishing.

I could jump ship, try to maintain Skipper on a diet of beans and biscuits, or I could invent my own shipboard recipes that would work on a slightly leaky but loved wooden boat with questionable refrigeration and no on-board electrical power.

Or I could take a leaf from Corrine Saunder's book: the first time we went cruising together, she said she intended to find the phone number of every pizza joint from Ile Perrot to Ottawa to Kingston and back to Ile Perrot. The only stipulation was that they had to guarantee delivery. With a VHF radio aboard *Otter*, making the calls wouldn't be a problem. Since pizza is such a nutritionally balanced food, and given that it is meant to be eaten with the fingers, the savings in dishes and dish detergent would certainly make it an ecologist's dream.

BREADS ~~~~~~~~~~~~~~~~~~~~~~~~~~~~

The first recipes I ever sold were a handful of boating recipes to *Recipes Only*. I am the product of a mother whose standard measurements were "enough" and "you'll know when it's right." Measuring ingredients on the boat was somewhat less than an exact science, especially since I worked on the theory that if one ingredient was missing, I could probably substitute something. Most things worked out.

However, the editor wanted exact amounts. I couldn't even use "dash," "pinch," or "sprinkle."

That was one of Jack's happiest winters. I whipped up batch after batch of scones and bannock and baking power biscuits, working with boating ingredients - margarine and canned evaporated milk. Jack was official tester and I would work backwards, trying to figure out what I put into each batch.

Jack was not unusually tall. He was slender. He discovered he could casually wipe out a batch of scones while he was chatting to me and wash them down, as it were, with a batch of bannock. Some evenings, he was surprised that he couldn't do justice to his dinner.

BANNOCK

This was designed to make over a campfire - and I suspect that ingredients and quantities were subject to change, depending on what was to hand.

2 cups (500 mL) flour
2 tsp (10 mL) baking powder
1/2 tsp (2 mL) salt

2 tbsp (30 mL) margarine
2/3 cup (150 mL) milk

Combine dry ingredients, rubbing the margarine into the flour, salt and baking power as for baking powder biscuits. Add enough milk to make a biscuit-like dough. Form into balls and flatten into rounds. Cook in an oiled frying pan over campfire coals or on a stove element. Turn several times while baking.

SCONES

1/2 cup (50 mL) margarine
1/3 cup (25 mL) white sugar
few grains of salt

1/2 cup (125 mL) canned
  evaporated milk, undiluted
1-1/2 cups (375 mL) white flour

Using a fork or whisk, cream margarine and sugar together in a medium-sized bowl. Add milk and stir into the margarine/sugar mixture. Mix flour and salt together in a separate bowl, then add to the creamed mixture. Stir until well mixed.

Roll out on a floured board to about 1/2 inch (1 cm) thick and cut into 8 to 10 rounds (use a floured drinking glass as a cutter) or take small chunks of dough and pat between your palms.

Put in pre-heated heavy pan over medium flame. Cover. (Does not have to be air tight. A lidded cast-iron frying pan works well.) Cook 10 minutes, turn, finish cooking through - another 5 or 10 minutes, depending on thickness. Makes 8 to 10. Recipe can be doubled. Serve warm or cold with a dollop of your favorite jam.

Variations: Add 1/2 cup (125 mL) raisins and 1 tsp (5 mL) cinnamon. • Add 1/2 cup (125 mL) finely chopped dates. • Open a can of strawberries in juice. Heat. Thicken with cornstarch or Veloutine. Follow directions on Veloutine package. When using cornstarch, mix a tbsp of cornstarch with a little cold water to make a smooth paste. Add hot liquid, a spoonful at a time, until the cornstarch mixture has been warmed up, then add to the strawberry juice. Adding cornstarch direct means lumps. Split the scones. Slather the bottom half with strawberries. Top with other half, more berries, and a shot of pressurized whipped cream topping.

IRISH SODA BREAD

This is a giant whole-wheat baking powder biscuit, more or less. It dries out fairly quickly but that doesn't present a problem because it has the potential to vanish very quickly. Cut in wedges and serve hot or cold.

1 cup (250 mL) whole wheat flour
2 cups (500 mL) white flour
1 tsp (5 mL) salt
1/4 cup (50 mL) brown sugar
1 tbsp (15 mL) caraway
   seeds
1/4 cup (50 mL) margarine
1 cup (250 mL) milk

In a medium-sized bowl, mix together dry ingredients. Add margarine and work in. Clean hands do a great job at this. Blend until all the little bits of margarine are coated with flour and the mixture is crumbly.

Add the milk. Stir until mixture comes away from the sides of the bowl. Dump onto a floured plate and knead for three minutes. Shape the ball of dough into a round loaf. Cut a deep X in the top.

Bake for about 45 minutes on your stove top in your disabled pressure cooker. Be sure to rest loaf on a cake rack to keep the bottom from burning.

Variation: Omit the caraway seeds and add a large handful of raisins or currants.

BAKING POWDER BISCUITS

2 cups (500 mL) white flour
4 tsp (20 mL) baking powder
1 tsp (5 mL) salt
1/3 cup (75 mL) margarine
3/4 cup (175 mL) milk,
   evaporated, diluted
1/2 cup (125 mL) raisins
   (optional)

Mix dry ingredients. Add the margarine. Blend with a fork or your finger tips until little bits of margarine are coated with flour and the mixture looks crumbly. Add milk. Stir with a fork. Add a little more milk if necessary to make a soft dough. If desired, dredge raisins in flour and add. Dump dough onto a floured plate. Knead dough 10 to 15 times. Pat out to about 3/4 inch (2 cm) thickness. Cut into 12 rounds or squares. Or drop by tablespoonfuls onto a small cookie sheet.

Cook on a rack in your pre-heated disabled pressure cooker for 10 to 15 minutes. Makes one dozen. Serve hot or cold.

CHEESE BUNS

Assemble ingredients for baking powder biscuits, then add 1/4 lb (100 g) cheese: sharp cheddar, Imperial or your choice
 Coarsely grate the cheese or chop into little pieces. Don't reduce to really small pieces - you want to encounter cheese nuggets inside the biscuits. Follow the regular baking power biscuit recipe. Before kneading, add the cheese. Continue with the baking power recipe.
 Variation: Add 1 tbsp (15 mL) parsley flakes and 1/2 tsp (2 mL) dry mustard with the cheese. Serve with soups or stews.

CINNAMON BUNS

These start out as baking powder biscuits. To bake, crowd them up against each other on a cake pan set on the rack in your disabled pressure cooker or any heavy pot with a well-fitted lid.

2 cups (500 mL) white flour
4 tsp (20 mL) baking powder
1 tsp (5 mL) salt

1/3 cup (75 mL) margarine
3/4 cup (175 mL) evaporated
  milk, undiluted

(*Filling:*)
1/2 cup (125 mL) brown sugar
1/4 cup (50 mL) margarine

2 tsp (10 mL) cinnamon

Mix dry ingredients. Add the margarine. Blend with a fork or your finger tips until little bits of margarine are coated with flour and the mixture looks crumbly. Add milk. Stir with a fork. Add a little more milk if necessary to make a soft dough. Dump dough onto a floured plate. Knead dough 10 to 15 times. Roll or pat the dough into a rectangle about 10 inches long.
 Mix the filling ingredients into a smooth paste. Spread filling onto dough. Starting at a long side, roll up fairly tightly, pinching the edges to prevent the roll from unwinding during cooking. Cut into 12 even rounds. Fit buns into a lightly oiled cake or pie tin. Bake in your pre-heated disabled pressure cooker or heavy pot for 10 to 15 minutes. Serve hot or cold.
 Variations: Add 1/4 cup (50 mL) raisins and/or pecans or walnuts to the filling mix, or use white sugar in place of brown.

QUICKIE SHORT CAKES

With an appropriate candle or two, these will do in a pinch as a birthday cake. In fact, they're a lot more fun than the standard cheap commercial chalk-and-sugar white birthday cake. They're really baking powder biscuits with a filling and topping.

2 cups (500 mL) white flour
4 tsp (20 mL) baking powder
1 tsp (5 mL) salt

1/3 cup (75 mL) margarine
3/4 cup (175 mL) evaporated
 milk, undiluted

1 can strawberries or blueberries
Veloutine - use according to package directions
pressurized whipped topping

Mix dry ingredients. Add the margarine. Blend with a fork or your finger tips until little bits of margarine are coated with flour and the mixture looks crumbly.

Add milk. Stir with a fork. Add a little more milk if necessary to make a soft dough. Dump dough onto a floured plate. Knead dough 10 to 15 times. Pat out to desired thickness and cut into 12 rounds or squares. Bake 12 to 15 minutes on a rack in your pre-heated disabled pressure cooker or heavy pot with a tight lid.

Meanwhile, empty the can of berries into second pot. Bring to a gentle simmer. Thicken as directed with Veloutine. Set aside to cool. Split cool biscuits in half. Put a large spoonful of berry mix on the bottom half. Cover with second half, add another spoonful of berries, squirt topping over the berries, and, finally, cap the whipped topping with another berry. Serve immediately, or the whipped topping will go flat and run all over everything..

Note: If you can't find Veloutine, thicken the berry liquid by mixing 1 tbsp (15 mL) of cornstarch with a little cold water, making a smooth paste. Add hot liquid, a spoonful at a time, to the cornstarch until that mixture has been warmed up, then add to the hot berries and simmer until the juice thickens, and loses the cornstarch "milky" look.

Variation: Sprinkle powdered sugar on top instead of whipped cream.

DEALING WITH STALE BREAD

Even our most determined attempts at practical shopping and stowing often left us holding a loaf of bread that was a day past its prime. Mouldy meant that it went into the garbage. We wouldn't even feed it to the local ducks and sea gulls. However, slightly stale was a challenge. Skipper dubbed our stale bread recipes "Vieux Pain," on the grounds that in cooking, a French name denotes a certain soupçon of elegance.

CINNAMON TOAST

Like most of the following recipes, this could be considered a breakfast dish. However, I would recommend it as a late-evening or gray-Sunday-afternoon snack.

sliced bread or biscuits
1/4 cup (50 mL) margarine

2 tbsp (30 mL) white or brown
  sugar
1 tbsp (15 mL) cinnamon

Toast bread slightly - stick a long handled fork through it and hold it over an open flame. Don't let it catch fire - slightly stale bread is a little trickier to toast than fresh.

Mix margarine, sugar and cinnamon into a smooth paste. Spread onto hot toasted bread. *or* Mix the sugar and cinnamon in a salt shaker, butter the bread, and sprinkle with the sugar/cinnamon mix.

QUICK CHEESE TOAST

1 small can evaporated milk,
  undiluted
1/2 cup (125 mL) grated cheese,
  hard cheddar or mozzarella

few grains of salt
sliced bread
sprinkle of paprika
  for colour

Heat milk in the top of a double boiler or in a small pot with a thick bottom. Add cheese and salt. Heat and stir until cheese is melted. Toast bread. (Pierce with a fork - toast over open flame.) Pour cheese sauce on toast, garnish with paprika, serve hot.

FRENCH TOAST

3 eggs
1/2 cup (125 mL) evaporated
  milk, diluted

few grains of salt
sliced bread
margarine for frying

Beat eggs until frothy. Add milk and salt. Soak bread in egg mixture for a few minutes. Turn to coat both sides.

Fry in margarine until golden brown. Turn once.

Serve with syrup, jam, marmalade or honey or with slices of ham for a quick lunch or supper.

PANCAKES~~~~~~~~~~~~~~~~~~~~~~~~~~~~~

POTATO PANCAKES

Nothing like a little vigorous potato grating to burn off a fair measure of "nowhere to find an overnight spot at a park island" Thousand Islands cruising frustration.

2 cups (500 mL) potatoes,
  peeled, grated
1 small onion, peeled, finely
  chopped (optional)

1 egg, well beaten
3 tbsp (45 mL) flour
1 tsp (5 mL) salt
3 tbsp (45 mL) oil

Drain grated potatoes well, then press and squeeze all the moisture out of them. Mix all ingredients together, beating well. Heat frying pan until a drop of water sizzles. Do not grease.

Drop batter by large spoonfuls onto pan. Spread into smooth circles. Makes 10 to 12 pancakes. Serve with applesauce or sour cream.

CORNMEAL PANCAKES

Any food that contained cornmeal was an automatic Skipper favourite. A slice of ham between two buttered thin cornmeal pancakes could be the ultimate sandwich.

1 cup (250 mL) water
1/3 cup (75 mL) cornmeal
1 cup (250 mL) evaporated
  milk, undiluted
1 cup (250 mL) white flour

1/2 tsp (2 mL) salt
2 tsp (10 mL) baking powder
1 egg, well beaten
1 tbsp (15 mL) margarine
oil for frying

Boil water. Add cornmeal, cook 5 minutes. Remove from heat. Slowly stir in milk. Mix dry ingredients together in separate bowl, then add to cornmeal mixture. Stir in the egg and the margarine. Heat frying pan until a drop of water sizzles. Grease with a few drops of oil. Dip batter with a large spoon. Batter will spread into circles. Cook until golden brown on one side, turn to cook the other side. Makes 8 to 12 generous pancakes. Serve with margarine, syrup, honey or jam.

PANCAKES

Short of fresh supplies? This recipe doesn't call for an egg. We liked pancakes for lunch when we knew we were going to goof off for the afternoon. They made us sleepy.

2 cups (500 mL) white flour
2 tbsp (30 mL) sugar
1/2 tsp (2 mL) salt
2 tsp (10 mL) baking powder

2 cups milk, fresh or
  diluted evaporated
1 tbsp (15 mL) margarine
oil for frying

Mix dry ingredients. Add milk slowly. Stir until smooth. Melt margarine. Add to batter. Heat frying pan until a drop of water sizzles. Grease with a small speck of cooking oil. (Margarine will burn.) Pour batter by spoonfuls onto pan, spreading slightly. Cook until top starts to look slightly dry and bubbles form, and bottom is nicely browned. Flip to cook other side. Makes 8 to 14 depending on size. Serve with margarine, honey, corn syrup, or fruit sauce.

FRUIT SAUCE

1 heaping tbsp (20 mL)
  cornstarch
2 tbsp (30 mL) lemon juice

1-14 oz can (398 mL)
raspberries, strawberries
or blueberries

Wet the cornstarch with spoonfuls of juice, stirring into a smooth paste so it doesn't go lumpy.

Combine all ingredients in saucepan. Bring just to the boil, then simmer, stirring frequently until thickened. Serve hot or cold.

BEVERAGES~~~~~~~~~~~~~~~~~~~~~~~~~

Without a fridge to hold cold drinks and lots of ice cubes, our boat beverages had to be interesting enough to compensate. It wasn't a hardship. We both learned to drink and enjoy plain water that ran cold only immediately after we filled the water tank. We experimented with all manner of fluids, knowing that, especially on a hot day, they were important.

Because of the garbage problem, we didn't like to carry single-serve boxes. There wasn't anywhere we could stow an opened can without having it spill. Glass juice jugs were stashed in an aft locker, padded so that they couldn't easily smash one another.

We discovered we liked hot Ovaltine made with milk and we both enjoyed fine herbal teas.

SUN TEA

4 tea bags
1 quart (1 litre) tepid water

4 or 5 whole cloves
2 cinnamon sticks

In the morning, put the tea bags (the better the quality, the better the tea) and spices into the jug of water. Lash securely to the mast. Leave all day.

If you have ice, make iced tea at night. Also good warm, not hot.

INGA'S PUNCH

I don't know where my daughter tumbled across this combination. I do know it became an instant hit. Mix and serve:

2 cups (500 mL) orange juice
1 large bottle ginger ale

1 large bottle pineapple-
  grapefruit juice

CRANBERRY COCKTAIL

When it's really hot, and fruit juice starts to feel too sweet, cut it with dry ginger ale, club soda, or 7 Up.

cranberry juice: equal parts to
  soda
1 apple, peeled and sliced
1 orange, peeled, in segments

dry ginger ale, club soda or
  7Up: use equal parts to juice
sprig of fresh mint

Pour juice over fruit. Set aside for an hour or two. Add soft drink, garnish with mint and serve.

ORANGE APRICOT DRINK

2/3 cup (150 mL) orange juice per serving
1/3 cup (75 mL) apricots, crushed or
  pureed

sprig of fresh mint

Combine juice and apricots. Let stand for an hour or more. Serve garnished with mint.

WHAT TO DO WITH WARM TOMATO JUICE

- Mix tomato juice and grapefruit juice, half and half.
- To each glassful of tomato juice, add 1 tbsp (15 mL) lemon juice, 1/2 tsp (2 mL) Worcestershire Sauce, a dash of salt and some freshly ground black pepper.
- To each glassful of tomato juice, add 1/2 tsp (2 mL) horse-radish. Garnish with parsley.

HOT MILK

This was the easiest way to soothe a ruffled Skipper. He liked his spices fresh and I discovered nutmeg can be grated easily on a standard cabbage grater.

1 cup (250 mL) milk per serving
1 tsp (5 mL) honey
whole cardamom pod

whole clove
small cinnamon stick
nutmeg for grating

Heat milk but do not boil. Boiled milk develops a perfectly nasty scum. Add honey, stir until dissolved. Add all spices except nutmeg. Heat for another moment or two, being careful not to let the milk boil. Fish out the whole spices. Pour milk into a big mug and dust with freshly grated nutmeg. Serves one.

SWEET LASSI

We are indebted for this recipe to a charming young waiter from an East Indian restaurant in Toronto. As I am not entirely sure his boss knew he was giving away the recipe, I shall leave it that, should he ever see this book, he knows to whom I refer....

Even friends who "hate yogurt" become addicted to this drink which is perfect with a curry dinner or at any other time, and is reason enough to head for shore for fresh yogurt and ice cubes.

Rose water can be found at specialty stores or in health food stores. A little goes a long way, and it keeps forever.

2 drops rose water
1/4 cup (50 mL) plain yogurt
2 heaping tbsp (30 mL) white sugar

1/4 cup (50 mL) water
1/4 cup (50 mL) milk

Mix all ingredients, shake well, and serve in tall glasses over lots of crushed ice. This recipe can be doubled and tripled at will, keeping in mind that you need very little rose water.

PASTAS AND RICE ~~~~~~~~~~~~~~~~~~~~~~~

As a mainstay, Skipper preferred steamed rice to potatoes or pasta. Rice on our erratic alcohol stove was a challenge, but manageable. The problem with pasta was our chronic shortage of water. At home, I rinse pasta under running water - not possible with our little tank without a gauge. The only way I knew the tank was low was when the pump started gulping air. We learned to take along a spare jug to carry us until we could fill the tank, but I wasn't into using quarts of water to rinse pasta.

PASTA

This applies equally to macaroni, spaghetti, noodles, Chinese Long Life noodles and novelty pasta shapes.

Use a large pot, and as much water as you can spare. Add to the water 1 tsp (5 mL) salt and 1 tbsp (15 mL) margarine or cooking oil. Bring water to a brisk boil.

Drop in a large handful of spaghetti or 1-1/2 cups (325 mL) macaroni. Add the pasta slowly, to keep water boiling. Stir pasta with a long-handled fork to separate strands and to keep it from forming into dense clumps.

Simmer to al dente, tender but firm. This takes anywhere from 8 to 12 minutes, depending on the type of pasta. Drain. Rinse with as much water as you can afford, to remove starchy overtones. Add 1 tbsp (15 mL) margarine. Stir. Reheat. Generous for 2, with some left over.

RE-FRIED MACARONI

I can never judge how much pasta to cook so I've learned ways to use up pasta leftovers.

Melt a large spoonful of margarine in frying pan. Add a dash of salt and some freshly ground black pepper. Stir in the cold macaroni. Stir and heat until the macaroni is hot and golden but not scorched.

Ladle into dishes. Grate some hard tangy cheese over the hot pasta. Leave for a minute or two so some of the cheese will melt before you serve it. Dress up with a sprinkle or a sprig of parsley.

Makes a useful side dish or a comfortable fast lunch served with a large glass of tomato juice and carrot sticks or radishes.

WHITE SPAGHETTI

Skipper liked this with a stew or, when he was tired and wanted something simple, he would make a meal of it. He maintained it was wonderful. It was certainly wonderfully simple.

small handful spaghetti per
  serving
2 tbsp (30 mL) margarine

1 tsp to 1 tbsp (5 to 15 mL)
  garlic flakes

Using as much water as you can spare, cook spaghetti according to package directions. Drain and rinse. Return spaghetti to pot. Toss with the margarine and garlic flakes. Heat gently and thoroughly.

MARC'S SPAGHETTI

I stole this great idea from Marc, our honorary French Canadian son. He claims to have stolen the idea from his uncle. Not knowing Uncle's name, I give the credit to Marc.

big handful of spaghetti
2 tbsp (30 mL) margarine
1 tsp (5 mL) garlic salt

2 tsp (10 mL) mixture of dried
  rosemary, thyme, parsley,
  oregano
salt and pepper

Cook spaghetti according to package directions in as much water as you can muster. Drain and rinse.

Return spaghetti to pot. Add margarine and herbs. Heat gently and thoroughly, tossing occasionally to keep spaghetti from sticking. Serves 2.

MACARONI AND TOMATOES

This is the macaroni dish I grew up on. As a child from a Saskatchewan farm, I didn't know people ate cheese with macaroni until I went away to college. This is still good eating on a cool summer's nights and it is high on my list of personal favourite foods. The recipe takes on a whole new life simply by substituting a can of herbed whole tomatoes for regular tomatoes. Tomato paste does not work.

2 cups (500 mL) dry
  macaroni
28 oz (796 mL) can of
  tomatoes

few grains each salt and pepper
2 tbsp (30 mL) margarine
1/2 tsp (2 mL) mixture dried basil,
  oregano, parsley, thyme, celery
  seed

In as large a pot as possible, simmer macaroni in as much water as available. Cook 10 to 15 minutes or until cooked but not soggy. Drain. Rinse in a minimum quality of water.

Return macaroni to pot. Add all the other ingredients using none, any, or all of the herbs suggested. Heat thoroughly to blend the flavours, but do not boil. Boiling wastes the vitamin content of the tomatoes.

Serve with hot scones or big slabs of brown bread and a simple salad. Serves 3 or 4 (or 2 with leftovers).

HIRONDELLE MACARONI AND CHEESE

This was one of our comfort foods on a cold and windy night. We'd serve it up with some fresh raw strips of carrot and zucchini or radishes cut in half and sprinkled with just a hint of salt. We'd end with fresh or canned fruit for dessert and leisurely cups of hot tea - and life would be good again.

2 cups (500 mL) dry
  macaroni
1/4 cup (50 mL) margarine
1 tbsp (15 mL) parsley flakes
1/2 cup (125 mL) evaporated
  milk, undiluted

1/2 to 1 cup (125 to 250 mL)
  chopped or grated cheese:
  hard cheddar or mozzarella
salt and freshly ground pepper
  to taste
fresh sprigs of parsley

In a large pot, using as much water as you can spare, simmer macaroni 10 minutes or until cooked but still firm. Drain, and rinse in a minimum quantity of water.

Return macaroni to pot. Add margarine and parsley flakes. Stir over medium flame until margarine is melted. Add milk and blend thoroughly. Add cheese and salt. Turn down heat. Stir while the cheese is melting. If the heat is too high, the cheese will overcook and get tough and stringy.

Garnish with fresh parsley and freshly grated black pepper. Serves three or four or feeds two nicely with the promise of cold macaroni left over for breakfast. (Crew doesn't like conventional breakfast choices.)

Variation: Add 1 heaping tsp (20 mL) curry powder when you add the cheese. Serve with a generous helping of chutney.

STEAMED RICE

I always cook extra rice. It keeps for a day, and fried rice is such great stuff. Leftover rice can also go into soups.

Rice does require a pot with a tight-fitting lid. You can fit a sheet of aluminum foil over the top of a pot, then put the lid on.

Before cooking, soak the rice in 2 to 4 cups of water for at least 30 minutes and much longer if possible. Soaking eliminates the sticky starchy problem and shortens the cooking time.

2 cups (500 mL) water	1 tsp (5 mL) salt
1 cup (250 mL) long grain white rice	1 tsp (5 mL) margarine

Bring salted water to a boil. Add margarine. Add rice and stir. Reduce heat and cook 20 minutes with lid on. Stir quickly with a fork. Replace lid and let rice sit covered for 5 minutes.

Note: My alcohol stove flatly refused to maintain the flame necessary to keep rice simmering. I learned to do "the rice ballet": heat up, heat down, pot off the burner, pot back on. Another solution was to simply cook the rice in scads of water and strain it when it was done.

Variation: Use fruit or tomato juice in place of all or part of the water. Add parsley or your favorite herbs to the cooking pot.

FRIED RICE

We considered this a complete meal with a little salad or some carrot or zucchini sticks on the side.

2 tbsp (30 mL) oil	1 can mushrooms, drained
1 onion, peeled, thinly sliced,	(discard liquid)
or chopped green onion	1 tbsp (15 mL) soy sauce
2 celery sticks, finely chopped	2 cups (500 mL) cold cooked rice

Heat oil in heavy pan. Add vegetables. Sauté until tender but crisp. Add soy sauce. Add rice. Mix well. Cook until rice is hot, stirring frequently. Serves 2 as a main dish.

Variations: Add a crumbled chicken or beef bouillon cube and a little water. • Add chunks of canned chicken. Handle canned chicken gently or it goes stringy. • Use Worcestershire sauce in place of soy sauce. • Add a heaping spoonful of dried vegetable flakes. • Omit soy sauce. Add a heaping spoonful of parsley flakes and a dash of salt and pepper.

EGGS ~~~~~~~~~~~~~~~~~~~~~~~~~~~~~~~~~

If you are not sure that the eggs are fresh, break them one at a time into a saucer. That's an easy way to ensure that you don't ruin a batch of something with one suspect egg.

Unwashed never-chilled eggs keep much longer than washed eggs that have been in long-term refrigerated storage. If you know a farmer with chickens, you might be able to get some truly fresh eggs.

Eggs created some of the Skipper and the Viking's most contentious moments. He liked his eggs in the morning, soft. "They're barely warmed up," the Viking would exclaim. She liked to know that eggs were not going to hatch while she was trying to eat them. When he cooked breakfast, he soft cooked all the eggs, presuming that the Viking would learn to eat them. She couldn't, and didn't. Besides, she liked eggs for supper, scrambled, mixed with interesting bits of mushroom and red pepper. Well done.

Fortunately, the Skipper and the Viking finally discovered that the earth could continue to revolve at roughly 24 hour intervals even though they each ate eggs the way they each most enjoyed them. They even learned to cook them properly for one another.

It was a defining moment in their relationship.

BACHELOR EGGS

An old favourite. For some odd reason, the smell of eggs frying in the morning is more than I can handle, but I like these.

margarine for frying
1 or 2 eggs per serving

sliced bread: white or brown,
a bit stale OK
salt and pepper to taste

Melt margarine in medium-sized frying pan. Break egg into pan. Let egg cook for just a moment, then cover with a slice of bread, pressing down to break the yolk if you like hard-cooked eggs. Turn once, to fry the bread-side an even golden brown. Sprinkle with a little salt and some freshly ground black pepper.

SCRAMBLED EGGS

1 or 2 eggs per serving
1 tsp (5 mL) evaporated undiluted
  milk per egg

1 tsp (5 mL) water per egg
2 tbsp (30 mL) margarine
salt and pepper to taste

Break eggs one at a time into a saucer then transfer to a bowl. Add milk and water. Beat until blended and frothy. Heat margarine to moderately hot, being careful not to let it burn. Pour in egg mixture. With a fork, toss eggs gently, allowing liquid to run to the bottom, until eggs are cooked to suit, from very moist to very dry. Sprinkle with a little salt and freshly grated black pepper.

Variations: Add a tablespoon (15 mL) or two of grated hard cheddar or mozzarella. • Add a little chopped onion and bits of ham. • Add 1 tbsp (15 mL) each parsley flakes and red pepper. • Add 1/4 cup (50 mL) canned or fresh mushrooms.

POACHED EGGS

Don't pack an egg poacher. It just takes up space. Use a small saucepan with a lid, and the metal rings that are used in home canning. Wash rings quickly in cold water so egg bits don't harden on them.

Skipper's favourite elegant quick meal was a bed of white rice with perfectly cooked poached eggs on one side and barely cooked spinach on the other, with a drop or two of lemon juice sprinkled on the spinach and freshly ground black pepper grated over everything. It looked as good as it tasted.

To poach eggs, put about 2 inches (5 cm) of water into a pot with a tightly-fitted lid. Bring to a boil, then turn down to a simmer. Put metal rings right side down into the water. Carefully break one egg at a time into a saucer. Slide each egg into a ring.

Poach covered for about 5 minutes or less for soft-poached, up to 7 to 10 minutes for hard-poached eggs. Use a flipper to lift the egg and the ring out of the pan. Once the egg is safely on the serving plate, remove ring.

SCRAMBLED EGGS WITH TOMATO AND BASIL

oil for cooking
2 chopped tomatoes or 2/3 cup
  (150 mL) canned, drained
1 tsp (5 mL) basil

1/2 tsp (2 mL) sugar
salt and pepper to taste
4 eggs, well beaten
2 tbsp (30 mL) water

Heat oil to medium heat. Add tomatoes, basil, sugar and salt. Cook until tomatoes are soft and hot. Beat eggs and water. Pour gently into tomato mixture, stirring constantly. Cook to desired consistency. Serve hot. Serves two.

HORS D'OEUVRES, APPETIZERS, CANAPÉS

We usually had the smallest boat, so when we met people on the Thousand Islands Park islands, we usually invited them for a cuppa, rather than an evening meal. As we did not have standing headroom, the time to have visitors was when we could all sit out in our roomy cockpit.

But what to nibble on with coffee or a drink? One short-order trick was to dig out a can of baby clams, drain them well, and offer guests a bowl of clams and a plate of crackers.

A second option was to dig out the jar of hot Salsa and box of Vegetable Thins. We could always find some offering that beat stale peanuts or limp vinegar potato chips.

CHICKEN CANAPÉS

margarine for frying
4 or 5 slices of bread
1 can chicken
1/4 cup (50 mL) slivered or
  chopped almonds
1/4 tsp (1 mL) celery salt
few grains salt and pepper
evaporated milk, undiluted:
  enough to moisten chicken

In margarine, fry bread until golden brown, one side only. Cut into triangles or squares. Mix all other ingredients with enough milk to make a spreadable mixture. Mound on untoasted side of bread.

SHRIMP COCKTAIL

lettuce or cabbage leaves to
  line bowl
1/2 cup (125 mL) ketchup, chili
  sauce or medium salsa
3 tbsp (45 mL) lemon juice
few drops Worcestershire sauce
salt and pepper to taste
4 oz (113 mL) can shrimp,
  drained
crackers

Line serving bowl with lettuce or cabbage leaves.

Mix ketchup, lemon juice, Worcestershire sauce, salt and pepper. Set aside for an hour. Add shrimp. Toss gently.

Heap shrimp mix into bowl. Serve as a dip with crackers.

AVOCADO AND HAM

2 or 3 cabbage leaves, red
  or green
1 or 2 avocados

1-2 tsp (15-30 mL) oil
1-2 tsp (15-30 mL) lemon juice
1-1/2 lb (680 g) canned ham
toothpicks

Line a serving bowl with cabbage leaves.

Peel avocado(s). Cut into cubes. Toss gently with oil and lemon. Coat well.

Cut ham into cubes. Put a toothpick through each cube. Pile up on cabbage leaves.

LEMON SAUCE

Company for morning coffee? Whip up a batch of baking powder biscuits. Serve hot or cold, slathered with this tangy alternative to jam.

1/2 cup (125 mL) sugar
1 tbsp (15 mL) cornstarch
1 cup (250 mL) water

2 tbsp (30 mL) lemon juice
2 tbsp (30 mL) margarine
few grains freshly grated nutmeg

Mix sugar and cornstarch. Slowly add cold water. Bring to a boil. Turn down heat. Simmer 5 minutes or until thick and clear. Remove from heat. Add lemon juice, margarine and nutmeg. Stir until well blended. Store in a clean sealed jar.

SOUPS, DUMPLINGS, CORN BREAD ~~~~~~

Once upon a time, the Skipper and the Viking were passionately attached to a certain brand of elegant packaged cream soups. A meal in a pot they were, served up with a slab of corn bread or a baking powder biscuit and some fruit. Then, one day, as the Viking sucked up her third or fourth spoonful, she dropped the spoon and grabbed her head. Skipper quickly checked the package ingredients. As he suspected, MSG, migraine delight.

As they sailed away happily ever after, the Skipper and the Viking vowed to always read cans and packages very carefully. As those three letters turned up more and more often, the Viking accepted a dose of reality and learned quick ways to make soup on board. (Simmering soup for four hours underway in rough weather on an alcohol stove that enjoys running out of fuel was not one of their favourite Olympic sports.)

INSTANT "VEGETABLE" SOUP

2 beef bouillon cubes
3 cups (750 mL) water
1/2 cup (125 mL) dried vegetable flakes

2 tsp (10 mL) each celery seed, parsley flakes

Crumble bouillon cubes, add to water, bring to boil. Add all other ingredients. Simmer for 10 to 15 minutes or until vegetable flakes are soft, not mushy. Could add bits of leftover vegetables, pre-cooked rice, pasta or dumplings at last minute. Serves 4.

DUMPLINGS

1 cup (250 mL) flour
2 tsp (10 mL) baking powder
1/2 tsp (2 mL) sugar

1/2 tsp (2 mL) salt
1/2 cup (125 mL) milk

Use a pot with a close-fitting lid. Mix dry ingredients. Add milk slowly, stirring, to make a soft batter. Drop by spoonfuls over the soup. Cover. Steam for 10 to 15 minutes. Makes 4 to 6 dumplings.

119

POTATO SOUP

There's something really satisfying about potatoes. This soup is quick enough and thick enough to make when you are in a moving galley and want to make something hot and satisfying. In the process, boil water and decant it into Thermos bottles for hot drinks later. The 3 or 4 servings can translate into 2 servings each for a cold and hungry Skipper and First Mate.

18 oz (540 mL) can potatoes
1 medium onion, peeled, thinly
  sliced
2 tbsp (30 mL) margarine

1 tsp (5 mL) celery seed
1-1/2 cups (385 mL) evaporated
  milk and same amount water
1 tsp (5 mL) parsley
freshly ground black pepper

Boil potatoes and onion in the potato liquid for 5 minutes. Drain potatoes and discard liquid. Dump potatoes back into pot. Add margarine and celery seed. Mash or beat potatoes into a smooth paste. Mix evaporated milk and water. Over low flame, add mixture to potatoes slowly, stirring constantly. Heat thoroughly without boiling. Just before serving, sprinkle with parsley and grate fresh black pepper on top. Serve in big mugs. Serves 3-4.

TOMATO SOUP

Homemade tomato soup is better than canned soup and doesn't take any longer to make. On board, it solves the problem of what to do with tomatoes bashed about in rough weather. This can be made from fresh milk, evaporated milk diluted with an equal amount of water, or reconstituted powdered milk.

3 cups (750 mL) milk
1 cup (250 mL) tomatoes,
  fresh chopped or canned
few grains sugar

1 tsp (5 mL) salt
1/2 tsp (2 mL) freshly ground
  pepper
sprig of parsley or dried flakes

Heat milk, then add tomatoes. Add other ingredients, stir to mix. Bring just to the boiling point, then turn down the burner. Simmer until thoroughly hot, not boiled. (Boiling will create scum on the soup. Not nice.) Garnish with parsley. Serves 3 or 4.

CORNMEAL BREAD (CORNBREAD)

If you didn't pack your muffin pan, you might like to try this version of cornmeal bread. Bake it in a shallow buttered pan that will fit onto the rack in your disabled pressure cooker. Bake about 20 minutes. Use fresh milk, reconstituted powdered milk or evaporated milk diluted half and half with water.

3/4 cup (175 mL) cornmeal
1 cup (250 mL) flour
1 tbsp (15 mL) baking powder
3/4 tsp (3 mL) salt

1 cup (250 mL) milk
1 egg, well beaten
2 tbsp (30 mL) margarine, melted

Mix dry ingredients. Add milk, egg and shortening. Mix. Bake 20 minutes. Makes 12 squares.

LENTILS, MONASTERY STYLE

This recipe came from a Montreal friend, Sue Lodwick. She insists that, served with a glass of milk, this is a totally balanced nutritious meal. However, she also recommends serving cornmeal muffins.

Don't try this underway in stormy weather. Cooking time is 45 minutes.

You can prepare everything ahead of time, but don't start cooking until you are safely anchored or docked for the night.

1/4 cup (50 mL) cooking oil
2 large onions, peeled and
  chopped
1 small carrot, peeled and diced
1/2 tsp (2 mL) thyme
1/2 tsp (2 mL) marjoram
1 tbsp (15 mL) parsley

2 cups (500 mL) fresh tomatoes,
  chopped, or 19 oz (549 mL) can
3 cups (750 mL) water
1 cup (250 mL) dried lentils,
  washed
2 chicken bouillon cubes,
  crumbled

In a large pot, heat the cooking oil. Add onions and carrots, stir and cook until the onion is transparent. Add the thyme and marjoram and cook 1 more minute. Add the rest of the ingredients and cook for 45 minutes, stirring occasionally. Serves 4 to 6.

SALVAGE VEGETABLE SOUP

This is an empty-the-hammock soup. The stock is made from a bouillon cube and almost any limp vegetable. It is strained, the stock vegetables are discarded, and fresh or dried vegetables are added and cooked until just tender.

1 quart (1 L) water
2 bouillon cubes: beef, chicken or
  vegetarian
assorted limp vegetables: carrots,
  cabbage, celery, potatoes,
  onions, tomatoes, parsley
1/2 tsp (2 mL) pepper

1 tbsp (15 mL) dried
  parsley flakes
1/3 cup (75 mL) dried
  mixed vegetable flakes
1 celery stalk
1 green onion, minced
salt to taste

Trim brown or wet spots from wilted vegetables. Chop vegetables into small pieces. Add with bouillon cubes to the water, bring to a boil, turn down the heat and simmer, covered, for one hour. Strain, saving liquid and discarding vegetables.

Add pepper, parsley, vegetable flakes, celery and onion. Bring to a boil again, turn down the heat, and simmer, covered, for 15 minutes. After a few minutes of simmering, taste and add salt as needed. Serves 3 or 4.

Variations: Add a couple of spoonfuls of rice or egg noodles with the vegetables flakes. Don't use very much. Rice swells and will take over the soup if given half a chance. Adjust seasoning by adding a little more salt and 1 tsp (5 mL) celery seeds. • Add leftover cooked vegetables, chopped into cubes, at the very end of the cooking time. Heat through. Do not boil. • Sprinkle with canned chow mein noodles just before serving.

MULLIGATAWNY SOUP

This takes a little time and patience because the vegetables need to be rubbed into a smooth paste. However, served with a salad, it's a complete meal. Besides, the galley smells wondrously fine for hours.

1/4 cup (50 mL) margarine
1 onion, peeled and diced
1/4 cup (50 mL) grated carrot
1 apple, peeled, cored, sliced
1/3 cup (75 mL) flour
1 quart (1 L) water
chicken bouillon cubes,
 crumbled

1 cup (250 mL) tomatoes,
 fresh or canned
1 tsp (5 mL) curry powder
1/2 tsp (2 mL) nutmeg
2 whole cloves
2 tbsp (30 mL) dried green
 pepper
salt and pepper to taste
4 oz (113 g) canned chicken

Melt margarine in heavy pot. Add the vegetables and the apple, cook until brown. Add the flour, stir until smooth. Add seasonings, tomatoes, water, chicken cubes. Bring to a boil, turn down heat, simmer for 1 hour.

Strain to separate vegetables from stock. Put vegetables into strainer over a bowl, stir and rub them with the back of a wooden spoon until they make a smooth paste. Return vegetable paste to soup stock. Add chicken. Simmer a few more minutes. Serves 3 or 4. Can be made with drained canned vegetables.

CORN CHOWDER

Hot soup and a slice of thick bread with a handful of dates or figs for dessert was, as far as the Skipper and the Viking were concerned, about the quickest and most soothing of all easy meals. This chowder is made quickly and easily from canned vegetables. However, if you have any leftover cooked potatoes around, use them. If using onion flakes, add them to liquid.

2 tbsp (30 mL) margarine
1 small onion, peeled, thinly
 sliced, or 2 tbsp (30 mL) flakes
1 can potatoes, drained, diced
14 oz (398 mL) can cream-style
 corn

1-1/2 cups (375 mL) milk
1-1/2 cups (375 mL) water
freshly ground black pepper
garnish: sprig of parsley
 parsley flakes or chopped
 green onion

Melt margarine in medium-sized pot. Add onion, cook a few moments until golden and translucent. Add potatoes, stirring briskly. Add corn, milk and water. Simmer 10 minutes. Do not boil. Add salt if necessary. Garnish just before serving. For 3 or 4.

DRESSINGS AND SALADS ~~~~~~~~~~~~~~

Mayonnaise belongs in a fridge once it is opened. However, there are other interesting dressings that can be made on board in minutes. Use your favourite oils and vinegars. Options listed are only suggestions.

FRENCH DRESSING

Basic recipe. There are as many variations as there are salads.

1/2 cup (50 mL) oil
1 tbsp (15 mL) plain or herb
  vinegar or lemon juice

1/2 tsp (2 mL) salt
bit of freshly ground pepper

Shake ingredients until well blended, using a small bottle with a tight fitting lid.

HONEY DRESSING

Try this with cabbage salad or Waldorf Salad.

1 heaping tbsp (20 mL) liquid honey
1 very full tbsp (20 mL) lemon juice
1/2 tsp (2 mL) salt

few grains paprika
  (optional)
1/4 cup (50 mL) oil

Beat honey, lemon, salt, and paprika. Add oil, a little at a time, beating constantly.

SWEET AND SOUR SALAD DRESSING

3 cups (375 mL) carrots and
  onions or cabbage and onions,
  shredded
1/2 cup (125 mL) white sugar
1/3 cup (75 mL) oil

1/3 cup (65 mL) white or
  herb vinegar
1 tsp (5 mL) mustard
1 tsp (5 mL) celery seed
1 tsp (5 mL) brown sugar

124

Grate carrots, shred cabbage, peel and thinly sliver onions.

Mix white sugar with vegetables and set aside for an hour. Meanwhile, using a small jar with a tight-fitting lid, shake remaining ingredients.

Toss dressing and vegetables together and let sit for an additional few minutes before serving.

SWEET AND SOUR MAYO

According to this recipe's source, a Canadian Power Squadron member and reader of Port Hole, Sweet and Sour Mayo comes from a seminar on living aboard without food refrigeration in the tropics. It will keep for six weeks at room temperature.

1 can sweetened condensed milk
1/4 cup (125 mL) cider vinegar

1-2 tsp (5-10 mL) dry
  mustard
1 tsp (5 mL) salt

Pour milk into clean jar. Pour vinegar into empty milk tin. Add mustard and salt to vinegar and mix. Add vinegar mixture to the milk in the jar. Put lid on jar and shake until mixture clabbers. Store covered.

CANNED MILK DRESSING

2 tbsp (30 mL) white sugar
3 tbsp (45 mL) vinegar
1/2 tsp (2 mL) salt
3 tbsp (45 mL) condensed milk

1 tsp (5 mL) celery seed
  (optional)
1/2 tsp (2 mL) dry mustard
  (optional)

To mix thoroughly, shake all ingredients in a small tight-lidded jar.

TOSSED SALAD

According to tradition, tossed salad should never be dressed with anything but oil and vinegar or lemon juice and herbs.

Besides the leafy greens, the tossed salad can contain strips of carrot, white turnip, zucchini, broccoli stalks, radishes, chopped onions, cauliflower or broccoli flowerets.

Select two or three different greens. Chose by flavour or colour or by discovering what won't last long in the fresh produce hamper. Wash the greens, dry them in a terry towel. Shred them by hand. Pour on 1 tbsp (15 mL) oil for a salad that will feed four people.

Toss patiently over and over again, up to 30 times, until all the leaves are coated with oil. This seals in freshness and vitamins.

Now add 1 tbsp (15 mL) vinegar, herb vinegar, lemon juice or lime juice. Add salt, freshly ground black pepper, cumin, dill, celery seed, or any favourite herb.

Toss again, 10 or 15 times.

CARROT SALAD

Carrots are my favourite on-board vegetable. They are the easiest to carry and store without refrigeration. When they go limp they can be used in soups and stews. They're bright and cheerful, they don't need fancy treatment, and they're versatile.

The carrot salad recipe is also versatile. Carrot/raisin happens to be my all time favourite and I could eat it every day. The salt and lemon juice keep the carrots from turning brown. Vinegar does as well. Salt isn't absolutely necessary.

4 carrots, peeled and grated
few drops lemon juice or lemon
  concentrate or vinegar

pinch of salt
1 tsp - 1 tbsp (5 mL - 15 mL)
  white sugar, to taste

126

Sprinkle grated carrots with lemon juice or vinegar and salt. Toss to coat carrots with lemon juice. Set aside for 15 minutes or more. Add sugar. Toss. Let sit for a few more minutes. Serve. Makes 4 generous servings.

Variations: Add 1/2 cup (125 mL) raisins to carrots. • Add 1/2 cup (125 mL) salted peanuts or cashews. • Add 1/2 cup (125 mL) very finely sliced cucumber or zucchini.

COLESLAW

1 small head of red and/or green cabbage, shredded, grated or finely sliced	1/2 tsp (2 mL) celery salt or salt and few grains of celery seed
2 tbsp (30 mL) white sugar	3 tbsp (45 mL) condensed milk
3 tbsp (45 mL) vinegar	

Prepare cabbage. Shake sugar, salt, vinegar, and milk in a small bottle until blended. Toss cabbage with dressing. Serves 4 to 6.

Variations: Add any combination of 1/2 cup (125 mL) grated carrots, peeled and chopped apples or drained canned pineapple. • For a children's party, add 1/2 cup (125 mL) pineapple chunks and a handful of colored miniature marshmallows. Dress with dressing as given or with pineapple juice mixed with a little lemon juice.

GREEN PEA SALAD

2 cups (500 mL) cooked fresh peas	1 green onion, sliced
1/4 cup (125 mL) cheddar cheese, cubed	1/2 cup (125 mL) celery or zucchini, chopped
1 to 4 tbsp (15 to 60 mL) salad dressing	1 tbsp (15 mL) sugar
	salt and pepper

Cook peas. Drain and cool. Add cheese, onion and celery. Add just enough salad dressing (Sweet and Sour Mayo, Canned Milk Dressing or Waldorf Salad Dressing) to moisten. Add salt, pepper and sugar. Serves 4.

127

WALDORF SALAD

Use pecans rather than walnuts. Walnuts go rancid very quickly, especially on board a warm, humid boat. Serves 4-6.

2 tbsp (30 mL) white sugar
3 tbsp (45 mL) vinegar

3 tbsp (45 mL) condensed milk
1/2 tsp (2 mL) salt

4 apples, washed, peeled,
  chopped

1/2 cup (125 mL) pecans
3-4 leafy celery stalks, sliced

Mix or shake sugar, vinegar, milk, and salt until sugar dissolves. Prepare apples and toss with dressing immediately to prevent browning. Add celery and pecans. Could use Honey Dressing.

POTATO SALAD

When I was a teenager spending wonderful summer days at Leslie Beach, Fishing Lake, before it became a popular resort, my girlfriends and I lived on potato salad, cold canned beans, Dad's oatmeal cookies and Kool Aid.

If you use hard-boiled eggs, don't add them until just before you serve this, then throw out leftovers. Or you can slice hard-boiled eggs over each individual serving.

(dressing)
2 tbsp (30 mL) vinegar
1 tsp (5 mL) salt
2 tbsp (30 mL) oil

1 tsp (5 mL) paprika, reserving
  some for garnish
freshly ground black pepper

4 potatoes, cooked, cooled,
  peeled, sliced (or use
  canned)
3 radishes, thinly sliced

1 or 2 green onions, sliced
2-3 hard-boiled eggs, sliced
1 or 2 parsley sprigs, chopped,
  reserving some for garnish

Mix dressing in jar with a good lid. Shake until blended. Combiine vegetables and toss with dressing until mixed. At the last minute, add the sliced eggs. Garnish with parsley and paprika. Makes 4 to 6 servings.

HAM AND POTATO SALAD

This can be an entire meal, served with a glass of tomato juice and a baking powder biscuit, wedge of cornmeal bread or slice of brown bread.

(dressing)
1/2 tsp (2 mL) salt
1 tbsp (15 mL) sugar
1/2 tsp (2 mL) dry mustard

3 tbsp (45 mL) evaporated
  milk, undiluted
1/2 cup (125 mL) oil
2 tbsp (30 mL) vinegar

19 oz (540 mL) can potatoes,
  drained and cut into small cubes
1/2 cup (125 mL) ham, cooked,
  cubed
1 or 2 leafy celery stalks, thinly
  sliced

4 or 5 radishes
1 or 2 parsley sprigs,
  chopped
few grains pepper
2 hard-boiled eggs, sliced
  (optional)

To make dressing, add milk slowly to dry ingredients, mix, add oil, beat until smooth. Add vinegar. Beat until well blended.

Assemble all salad ingredients, reserving the eggs, if used, until just before serving. Toss salad ingredients and dressing.

PICKLED BEETS

Quick and effective. Make in the morning, serve for supper. Keep leftovers in a clean sealed jar.

1 cup (250 mL) white vinegar
1 cup (250 mL) white sugar
1 cup (250 mL) water

1 tsp (15 mL) salt
1 tbsp (15 mL) whole cloves
14 oz (398 mL) canned beets

Mix all ingredients except beets in a lidded pot. Cover. Bring to a boil. Simmer for 5 to 10 minutes. Meanwhile, drain beets. Pour hot liquid over beets. Leave until cool.

WARNING: Beet juice stains everything in sight permanent bright red. Don't splash it around.

CAN SALAD

You have a big crowd to feed, and there's absolutely nothing fresh and inviting in your produce hammock. Can salad!

1/2 cup (125 mL) oil
2 tbsp (30 mL) white vinegar
1 tsp (5 mL) celery seed
salt to taste

1 tsp (5 mL) black pepper,
  freshly ground
1 tsp (5 mL) parsley, fresh
  chopped or dried flakes

14 oz (398 mL) can green beans
14 oz (398 mL) can kidney beans
14 oz (398 mL) can lima beans

19 oz (549 mL) can chick-
  peas
1 med. onion, peeled, sliced

In a jar or bottle, shake oil, vinegar and spices until blended. Drain beans and chick-peas. Mix with dressing. Add onions. Let sit for an hour or 2 before serving. For 8 to 10 generous servings.

Variations: Add a handful of your favourite cheeses, cubed. Or add a tomato or two, chopped fine.

MAIN DISHES WITH MEAT ~~~~~~~~~~~~

HAM IN RAISIN SAUCE

1/4 cup (50 mL) brown sugar
1 tsp (5 mL) dry mustard
1 tsp (5 mL) white flour
1/4 cup (50 mL) raisins
2 tsp (30 mL) white vinegar

1/2 cup (125 mL) water
1 inch (3 cm) fresh ginger root
  or 2-3 candied ginger cubes
2 slices ham, pre-cooked
1 small can pineapple slices

Raisin sauce: mix brown sugar, mustard and flour. Add raisins, vinegar and water. Simmer over low heat. Peel ginger root, slice into paper-thin slices, add to sauce mixture. Add ham to the sauce. Saving pineapple juice, arrange pineapple rings around ham. Simmer sauce until ham is hot and sauce begins to thicken, turning the ham at least once and watching the pineapple so that it turns golden brown, not black. Serve with rice made with pineapple juice as part of the cooking water. Serves 2.

Variation: Use pineapple chunks and cut ham into bite-sized pieces. Easy for children to manage.

FROM-THE-CANS CHILI

This recipe can be halved easily, but I like to make big batches of chili because it's standard feed-a-bunch fare, served in bowls with hot biscuits or crusty bread and salad. The longer you simmer it, the better it is.

A chemistry prof friend of mine whose advice I trust once told me that if there are sprays on tomatoes, they reach their most concentrated state in tomato paste. I now use ordinary canned tomatoes. Takes a little longer to thicken, but the idea of toxins in our stew doesn't add much to my culinary enjoyment.

2 large onions, peeled and sliced
1/8 cup (25 mL) green pepper,
  or 1 tbsp (15 mL) dried flakes
2 - 19 oz (549 mL) cans tomatoes
10 oz (284 mL) can mushrooms
2 - 14 oz (398 mL) cans kidney
  beans
2 large cans meatballs in gravy
2 or 3 bay leaves

1 tbsp (15 mL) each chili
  powder or crushed chilies,
  parsley, sweet basil, celery
  seed, oregano, whole or
  powdered cumin
1 inch (3 cm) ginger root,
  peeled and thinly sliced,
  or 1 tbsp (15 mL) dried
  ground ginger
salt and pepper to taste

Mix all ingredients in a large thick-bottomed pot, bring to a boil, turn down to simmer, and cook for at least 30 minutes, longer if possible. After 30 minutes, taste and adjust seasonings. It is the ginger root that give this chili its real kick.

Serve with crusty bread. Serves 4 to 6.

HERBED CRUSTY BREAD

1/4 cup (50 mL) margarine
1 tsp (5 mL) each dried chives,
  parsley and celery seed

loaf of bread, fresh or
  slightly stale

Mix herbs with margarine. Melt margarine slowly, take it off the heat and let it sit while you toast the bread.

Cut inch-thick (3 cm) slices of bread. Toast, using a fork, over a hot burner. Spread with margarine mixture. Toast more bread as needed.

CORNED BEEF HASH

1 can corned beef
1 can potatoes, drained, or 1
   cup (250 mL) leftover boiled
pepper (and salt to taste)

1 very small onion, chopped
   or 1 tsp (5 mL) dried onion
   flakes
margarine or oil for frying

Chop corned beef into small bits. Mash potatoes. Mix corned beef, potatoes, onion and pepper. Taste before adding salt - you might not need any.

Melt margarine in heavy frying pan. Spread hash evenly in pan. Cook slowly, about 20 minutes, until a brown crust has formed on the bottom of the pan, or stir during cooking to get crisp brown flecks spread throughout the hash.

HIRONDELLE STEW

This stew is fairly ordinary, but topped by cornmeal dumplings (recipe follows) this became another of Skipper's favourite boating meals. The big advantage of the stew is that all the ingredients come from cans or bottles. The recipe requires no thinking at all. For entirely brain-dead days, dumplings can be made from biscuit mix. A large glass of juice, an apple for dessert and voila! an instant meal with some genuine nutrition.

My mother insisted that corn and stew didn't mix. This might have been an attitude that came from the days when corn was home canned and sometimes ran the risk of botulism. I don't know. I just don't put corn in stew.

10 oz (284 mL) can mushrooms,
   drained
14 oz (398 mL) can lima beans
19 oz (340 mL) can chunky
   beef soup
14 oz (398 mL) can baby carrots

1 tbsp (15 mL) dried
   onion flakes
1/2 tsp (2 mL) parsley flakes
1/2 tsp (2 mL) celery seed
1/2 tsp (2 mL) thyme

Drain mushrooms and lima beans, discard liquid. Dump chunky soup and all remaining ingredients into medium-sized pot, adding the carrot liquid to the brew. Bring to simmer and heat for 20 minutes or long enough to blend flavours. Thicken with Veloutine if you want a stiffer gravy. Serves 3 or 4.

132

CORNMEAL DUMPLINGS

1 cup (250 mL) water
1/2 cup (125 mL) cornmeal
1 tsp (5 mL) salt
1/2 cup flour (125 mL)
1 tbsp (15 mL) baking powder

1 egg
1 tbsp (15 mL) margarine
   or oil
1 tsp (5 mL) onion flakes
few grains of pepper

Boil water in pot with tightly-fitted lid. Slowly add cornmeal and salt, cook 2 minutes. Remove from heat. Cool. Add flour and baking powder to cornmeal. Mix. Beat egg, add, mix well. Add oil, onion, pepper. With tablespoon, scoop up 4-5 dumplings, drop on top of simmering stew. Simmer, covered, 15 minutes.

CHICKEN SALAD

4 oz (113 mL) can chicken
1 green onion, sliced
1 leafy celery stalk, thinly sliced

small handful of unsalted
   almonds or cashews
salt and pepper to taste

(dressing)
1/2 tsp (2 mL) salt
1/2 tsp (2 mL) dry mustard
2 tbsp (30 mL) oil

1 tsp (5 mL) vinegar
3 tbsp (45 mL) evaporated
   milk, undiluted

To the dry dressing ingredients add the oil, vinegar and milk, beating until smooth. Add all salad ingredients. Serve as salad for 3, or make 3 generous pita sandwiches.

CURRIED CHICKEN SALAD

Chicken Salad Dressing
4 oz (113 mL) can chicken
1/2 or small zucchini, thinly
   sliced
1 celery stalk, cleaned, sliced

1 apple, peeled, cored,
   thinly sliced
1 tsp (5 mL) curry powder
1 green onion, sliced
few grains cayenne pepper

Make Chicken Salad Dressing (above). Mix all salad ingredients, stirring to mix in the curry and cayenne. Toss with dressing. Serves 3. Could stuff into 3 pitas and serve as sandwiches.

VEGETABLES ~~~~~~~~~~~~~~~~~~~~~~~~~~~

All our vegetables swinging in the hammock went limp a little faster than in the fridge at home. We had to spend proportionally more time to dress them up.

ONE-POT VEGGIES

1 small turnip	1/4 cup (50 mL) margarine
2 or 3 carrots	1 tbsp (15 mL) brown sugar
2 or 3 potatoes	salt and pepper to taste

Peel all vegetables, chop into small pieces, and boil in one pot in a minimum of water for 20 minutes or until soft enough to be mashed. Drain. Mash. Add margarine and brown sugar and mash some more. Salt and pepper to taste. Serve hot to 2 or 3.

BASIL 'N' CARROTS

Simple, but very special

1 carrot per serving	1-2 tbsp (15-30 mL)
2-3 tbsp (30-45 mL) margarine	dried basil
	salt and pepper to taste

Scrape carrots and slice lengthwise. Boil in a minimum of water until tender - 15 to 25 minutes. Drain and return carrots to cooking pot. Add margarine and basil, stir until margarine is melted, then cook gently for 3 or 4 minutes at very low heat. Season with salt and pepper. Serve hot.

DRESS-UP BEANS

Herbed canned green beans contain MSG, which gives me migraines. As frozen vegetables are more of a challenge than we wanted on an iceless boat, we invented these.

14 oz (398 mL) can green beans
1 tbsp (15 mL) dried red pepper
1 tbsp (15 mL) celery seed

1 tbsp (15 mL) margarine
1/4 tbsp (1 mL) rosemary,
  crumbled

Combine all ingredients. Set aside for half an hour so that the beans can absorb some of the flavour of the herbs. Simmer over very low heat, very gently, for 5 minutes to combine flavours. Drain, toss with a little margarine. Serve hot to about 3.

SWEET AND SOUR RED CABBAGE

1 small head red cabbage,
  shredded
1/2 cup (75 mL) brown sugar

1/4 cup (50 mL) vinegar
1/4 cup (50 mL) margarine

Cook cabbage in an inch or two of water to which you have added the brown sugar. Cook 8 to 12 minutes, until cabbage is tender but not limp and soggy. Drain. In serving bowl, toss with margarine and vinegar. Serve immediately. Serves 4.

OLD-FASHIONED STEWED TOMATOES

My mother made these, of a winter's night, from her own home-grown, home-canned tomatoes. I loved them. This is still one of my most important food groups. Serve this with scrambled eggs - or make a meal out of it on those days when the weather is cranky and you want to snuggle down in a cozy bunk with some good audio tapes, a book and something soothing to eat.

19 oz (540 mL) canned tomatoes
2 or 3 slices brown bread, fresh
  or stale

a few parsley flakes
salt and pepper

Heat the tomatoes but do not boil. (Don't destroy any stray vitamin that might have survived processing.)

Tear the bread into bite-sized pieces. Add enough bread to soak up almost all the juice. Sprinkle on the parsley. Stir gently so you don't break up all the tomatoes. Add salt and pepper to taste. Serve hot.

STEAMED VEGETABLES

There are few vegetables (excepting turnips) that don't benefit from steaming rather than boiling. Steaming retains flavour, colour and vitamin content. Small potatoes in their skins are wonderful. All green vegetables stay greener. Carrots take time but the wait is worth the results.

Prepare vegetables as for boiling. Use a pot with a tightly fitted lid or cover the pot with aluminum foil before you put on the lid. Pour an inch or two of water into the pot. Bring to a boil.

Arrange vegetables on the steamer. (Mine is three-legged and tips over if I overload one side. If you're out at anchor and there isn't a steamer handy, take two or three of the metal sealer rings that you use for poaching eggs, set them on the bottom of the pot, and arrange your vegetables on top, on an island above the water. Simple. Cheap. It works.) Jam on the lid and cook vegetables until tender but not limp. Toss with a little bit of margarine or melt a bit of grated cheese on top or sprinkle with dried grated cheese or freshly ground black pepper.

COMPANY MUSHROOMS

1 can mushroom pieces and stems	2 tbsp (30 mL) soy sauce
	2 tbsp (30 mL) margarine

Combine and heat thoroughly.

MEATLESS MAIN DISHES ~~~~~~~~~~~~~~~

My expert on vegetarian eating, son Joe, follows a strict macrobiotic diet, but does not call himself a vegetarian because he does eat fish. "Not growing from the ground, it is not a vegetarian food." Veggans do not eat any animal product, such as eggs and dairy. Vegetarians do eat eggs and dairy products.

Macrobiotic diets are also popular. They include less protein and more carbohydrate, and include fish but no raw vegetables. The deal here, Joe says, is not humanitarian but to eat what digests well. Red meat and raw vegetables don't, fish and steamed vegetables do.

If you have a vegetarian friend or family member coming aboard, don't panic. Around our house, the complaint from the vegetarians is that the non-vegetarians are eating up all their special food. Besides, on our boat, without refrigeration, vegetarian meals simply made life easier.

PUNJABI CHANA

Proof of how tasty a vegetarian dish can be.

1 small onion, minced
1 inch (3 cm) fresh ginger root, peeled and thinly sliced
2 tbsp (30 mL) oil
1 can chick-peas or garbanzo beans

1/2 tsp (2 mL) each turmeric powder, garlic powder, cumin, garam masala, coriander
few drops lemon concentrate (plastic squeeze lemon)

Peel and slice onion and ginger root. Cook in oil in a medium-sized frying pan at very low heat for 5 minutes. Add all the spices, Cook another 5 minutes.

Drain the chick-peas. Save about 1/2 cup (125 mL) liquid. Add chick-peas (chana) and liquid to the spice mix. Simmer 10 to 15 minutes until flavours are cooked into the beans but the beans are not mushy. Before serving, sprinkle liberally with lemon juice. Serve with white or brown steamed rice or over noodles.

CORNMEAL BREAD (CORNBREAD)

3/4 cup (175 mL) cornmeal
1 cup (250 mL) flour
1 tbsp (15 mL) baking powder
3/4 tsp (3 mL) salt

1 cup (250 mL) milk
1 egg, well beaten
2 tbsp (30 mL) margarine, melted

Mix dry ingredients. Add milk, egg and shortening. Mix. Bake 20 minutes in 8 by 8 greased shallow pan. Will cook nicely stove top. Cover pan tightly; put a metal grill between the stove top element and the pan. Makes 12 squares. Serve with chili.

NO-MEAT CHILI

2 large onions, peeled, sliced
2 stalks celery, cut in one-inch
  (3 cm) pieces
1 tsp (15 mL) each chili powder,
  parsley, oregano, sweet basil,
  celery seed, powdered or
  whole cumin
2 or 3 dried bay leaves

2 cans tomatoes
2 cans kidney beans
1 can mushrooms
1 inch (3 cm) fresh ginger
  root, peeled and sliced
salt and pepper to taste
1/8 cup (25 mL) dried
  green pepper flakes

Dump everything into a large thick-bottomed pot, bring to a boil, turn down to simmer, and cook for at least 30 minutes, longer if possible. Adjust seasonings if necessary.

Serve with thick slices or chunks of cornbread.

VEGETARIAN SPANISH RICE

Most of us think of Spanish Rice as a meat dish. However, we didn't carry ground beef aboard Hirondelle.

2 tbsp (30 mL) margarine
2 cups (500 mL) cooked brown
  or white rice, or 1 cup (250
  mL) dry
2 tsp (30 mL) dried onion flakes
  or 1 peeled, sliced onion, or 2
  green onions, minced
2 cups (500 mL) water
10 oz (284 mL) can mushrooms

19 oz (540 mL) can tomatoes
1-2 stalks leafy celery, sliced
  tbsp (30 mL) dried green
  pepper
1/2 tsp (2 mL) oregano
2 tsp (10 mL) chili powder
1/2 tsp (2 mL) basil
1/2 tsp (2 mL) celery seed
2 tsp (2 mL) parsley
salt and pepper to taste

Melt margarine in lidded frying pan. If using cooked rice, brown rice with onion, stirring frequently. Add all other ingredients. Stir, bring to a boil. Turn down flame. Cover frying pan. Simmer 10-15 minutes.

If using dry rice, simmer with all other ingredients, stirring frequently so mixture doesn't stick or burn, until rice is cooked, 30 minutes for white rice, up to 45 minutes for brown. Add more water or some tomato juice if necessary. Adjust seasonings.

Makes 4 or 5 servings.

138

FISH CAKES

1 small can salmon or any
  cooked fish
1 can potatoes or 1 cup
  (250 mL) boiled
1 egg, well beaten

2 - 3 tbsp (30 - 45 mL) flour
1 tbsp (15 mL) parsley
1 small onion, minced, or 1
  tbsp (15 mL) dried flakes
oil for frying

Drain salmon. Drain potatoes. Mash with a fork. Mix all ingredients but oil. Set aside for a few moments. On a floured board, form into four patties. Fry in oil until nicely browned and hot through. Turn once. Serve hot.

TUNA AND APPLE PITA BREAD FILLING

4 oz (113 mL) can tuna
1 small apple, grated
few drops lemon juice
2 tbsp (30 mL) nuts, unsalted,
  finely chopped

few drops evaporated milk,
  undiluted
salt and pepper to taste
3 or 4 pita bread

Drain and mash tuna. Add apple, lemon juice, nuts, enough milk to moisten, salt and pepper. Stuff into pita bread. Or serve as a salad.

SALMON SNACK IN PITA

4 oz (113 mL) can salmon
few drops lemon juice
3 or 4 radishes, thinly sliced
1 very small zucchini, thinly sliced

few drops evaporated
  milk, undiluted
salt and pepper to taste
3 or 4 pita bread

Mash salmon, juices and all. Add other ingredients. Stuff into pita bread.

QUICK CURRIES AND CONDIMENTS ~~~~~

Curry was unquestionably our favourite food. My first job as First Mate and Chief Cook was to adapt our curry recipes so we could make them on board *Hirondelle*.

CURRIED SHRIMP

1 apple
2 tbsp (30 mL) oil
1 small onion, peeled, sliced,
  or 3 tbsp (45 mL) dried
  onion flakes
1 tbsp (30 mL) curry powder
1/2 tsp (2 mL) turmeric
1/2 tsp (2 mL) salt
freshly ground black pepper

1 tsp (5 mL) each cumin seed,
  mustard seed, crushed
  cardamom seed
3/4 cup (175 mL) water
2 or 3 tbsp (25 mL) Veloutine
  for thickening if necessary
2 - 4 oz (113 mL) cans shrimp
few drops lime juice
  concentrate

Peel and core apple, cut into thin slices. Heat oil in medium-sized frying pan. Add onion and apple. Cook lightly. Add spices. Stir and cook until apple is soft. Add water. Simmer 10 to 20 minutes to blend flavours. If necessary, thicken slightly with Veloutine according to package directions. (Veloutine's advantage is that it can be added directly to hot liquid and it will not lump.)

Add shrimp. Heat thoroughly and gently. Just before serving, sprinkle generously with lime juice. Feeds 2 hungry sailors.

CURRIED CHICKEN FROM CANS AND JARS

2 tbsp (30 mL) oil
1 small onion or 3 tbsp (45 mL)
  or dried onion flakes
1 tbsp (30 mL) curry powder
1 tsp (5 mL) each turmeric,
  cumin seed, mustard seed,
  crushed cardamom seed
freshly ground black pepper
1/2 cup (125 mL) raisins

1 apple, peeled, cored, thinly
  sliced, or 1/2 cup (125 mL)
  applesauce
1 cup (250 mL) water
4 oz (113 mL) can of chicken
few sprigs parsley or
  1 tsp (5 mL) dried
small handful cashews
few drops lime juice concentrate

140

Note: There is no salt added because canned chicken is usually quite salty. Also, canned chicken falls apart easily, so don't add it until the last minute. Lift and turn it with a slotted spoon rather than stirring or it will break down and become stringy.

Heat the oil with the onions and green pepper. Add all the spices. Cook and stir for 3 or 4 minutes. Add applesauce or apple chunks and raisins. Cook and stir for another 3 or 4 minutes. Add the water and simmer for 10 or 15 minutes to blend the flavours. Break up the chicken, handling it carefully. Add to the curry mix and heat thoroughly without letting the mixture boil.

Just before serving, garnish with parsley, sprinkle generously with lime juice, and sprinkle the cashews on top. With rice, a salad and fresh fruit for dessert, this dish can serve three or four, but can easily be mopped up by two very hungry sailors.

CURRIED EGGS

This recipe title is a little misleading. It's the cream sauce that's curried, not the eggs. This was Skipper's all-time comfort food. When he was cold, sad, tired or his tummy hurt, this was the food he wanted. He had spent the war years in India, where he swam in sapphire blue lagoons and learned to enjoy authentic East Indian food, a acquired taste which he never lost.

1 or 2 eggs per serving	1-2 tsp (5-10 mL) curry powder
2 tbsp (3o mL) margarine	2 cups (500 mL) milk, whole or
2 tbsp (30 mL) flour	evaporated, diluted

Hard boil eggs. (Put eggs into cold water. Bring to boil. Turn down heat until just simmering. Simmer 10 to 25 minutes. *Or* turn off heat and leave eggs for 20 minutes or until water cools.)

Meanwhile, in a separate pot, melt margarine. Add flour, a little at a time, stirring constantly. Cook one minute. Add milk, a little at a time to avoid lumps, stirring constantly. Stir and cook for 2 to 3 minutes. Add curry powder, cook for a moment. Cover and keep warm. Drain eggs. Peel and cut in half. Pour curry sauce over eggs. Serve hot. Serve with steamed rice with a sweet chutney on the side. Serves 3 or 4..

PICKLED CARROTS

A good side dish for a curry meal, or any meal, for that matter.

2 medium carrots

1/2 tsp (2 mL) salt
1 tsp (5 mL) turmeric

Clean and peel carrots. Cut into long, thin strips. Sprinkle with salt and turmeric, mix well and set aside for two hours before serving. Will keep at least one day without refrigeration. (When the carrots go limp, chop and add to a soup or stew.) Serves 2.

QUICK CHUTNEY

Best after a month or two, so make at home one or two months before your cruise, and don't forget to take it along.

2 cups (500 mL) raisins
2 cups (500 mL) apples,
  peeled, cored, diced
1 large Spanish onion, peeled,
  sliced in thin rounds
1-1/2 cups (375 mL) white or
  brown sugar

1 inch (3 cm) fresh ginger
  root, peeled, thinly sliced,
  or 3-4 pieces of candied
  ginger minced, or 1 tsp
  (5 mL) ground dried
2 cups (500 mL) vinegar
1 tsp (5 mL) salt

Mix all ingredients in the heaviest pot you own. Bring to a boil then simmer 30 minutes, stirring frequently and watching that the mixture does not scorch. Use immediately or ladle into hot, sterilized jars. Seal. Let cool undisturbed. Check seals and store. Or ladle into freshly washed, hot jars, seal and keep refrigerated.

BASMATI RICE

Note: Basmati is the Queen of Indian rice, long grained, nutty, fragrant and expensive. It does have to be picked over and washed before cooking. A bag of Basmati often contains small stones and other impurities. Also, it should be washed 3 or 4 times before cooking, which means dipping into a precious boating water supply, making this a choice for special occasions.

Note: Well-cooked tender fluffy rice requires a tightly fitted lid over a heavy-bottomed pot. If the lid on your best pot isn't a tight fit, cover the pot tightly with a layer of aluminum foil then put the lid on.

1-2/3 cups (425 mL) Basmati
  rice
2 tbsp (30 mL) margarine
1 tsp (5 mL) salt

2-1/3 cups (570 mL) water
  (will need extra for rinsing
  and soaking)

Pick over the rice, wash in 3 or 4 changes of water, drain. Soak for half an hour in 4 cups of water. Drain thoroughly. Discard water. Combine rice, salt, margarine and 2-1/3 cups water in a heavy-bottomed pot. Bring to a boil. Cover with a tightly fitted lid. Cook over very low heat for 20 minutes. Lift lid, stir gently and quickly with a fork and cover again. Cook for 5 or 10 more minutes. Let stand for 5 minutes before serving.

CARROT AND ONION SALAD

Another simple salad that goes well with curry.

2 small carrots
1 medium onion

1/4 cup (50 mL) white vinegar
1/4 cup (50 mL) white sugar
1/4 tsp (1 mL) salt

Scrape carrots, cut lengthwise into long slender strips. Peel onion, slice into thin rings.

Mix sugar, vinegar and salt in a small bowl, stirring to dissolve sugar. Add carrots and onion slices. Soak for as long as possible. If desired, drain off and discard excess liquid before serving. Feeds 2.

WHITE SAUCE ~~~~~~~~~~~~~~~~~~~~~~~~~~~~

Skipper enjoyed cooking. His specialties were anything with rice, especially leftover rice, anything with a curry base and anything with a white sauce.

SKIPPER'S CREAMED CELERY

This was a spur-of-the-moment invention one night when Skipper had galley duties. We fell in love with it. There's something warm and old-fashioned about this, like being wrapped in a handmade patchwork quilt.

1 or 2 celery stalks, fresh or going limp, per serving	1 cup (250 mL) milk, fresh or evaporated, diluted
2 tbsp (30 mL) margarine	few grains salt and pepper
2 tbsp (30 mL) white flour	

Clean celery. If it's really stringy, cut away the worst bits. Cut into chunks that will fit your pot. Bring water to a boil, then turn down heat and simmer 10 to 15 minutes, so celery is cooked but still slightly firm.

Meanwhile, in a separate pot, melt margarine. Add flour, a little at a time, stirring constantly. Cook for one minute, stirring constantly. Add milk slowly, stirring to avoid lumps. Bring just to boil, turn down heat, simmer, stirring, for 2 minutes. Add a little more milk if sauce is too thick. Add salt.

Drain celery. Add celery to cream sauce and stir. Serve hot with a dusting of freshly grated black pepper. Will serve four, but two determined people can wipe this out.

CREAMED ONIONS

I'm not sure that I'd want to start boiling onions during a frontal low when I knew I wouldn't be able to air the cabin for a couple of days. On the other hand, these are really good with a slice of canned ham and some steamed rice or buttered noodles.

1 whole onion, peeled, per
  serving
2 tbsp (30 mL) margarine
2 tbsp (30 mL) flour
few grains of salt

1 cup (250 mL) fresh milk
  or evaporated, diluted
parsley, fresh or dried, for
  garnish
freshly ground black pepper

Simmer onions in water for at least 20 minutes. Onions take forever to cook.

Meanwhile, in a separate pot, melt margarine. Add flour, a little bit at a time, stirring constantly. Cook for one minute. Add milk, a little at a time, stirring constantly. Bring to a boil, then turn down to simmer. Cook 2 or 3 minutes, stirring constantly. Add a few grains of salt. Keep warm. Cover so that the white sauce does not develop a crust.

Drain onions. Add to the cream sauce. Serve hot, garnished with parsley and freshly ground black pepper.

WHITE SAUCE

Feel like having people over, and you don't want to spend hours in the galley? Make a salad and serve with creamed salmon, tuna or chicken on toast.

2 tbsp (30 mL) margarine
2 tbsp (30 mL) flour
salt and pepper to taste

1 cup (250 mL) fresh milk or
  evaporated, diluted

Melt margarine. Add flour. Stir and cook for one minute. Add salt and pepper. Add milk slowly, stirring constantly. Cook over low heat, stirring, for 2 minutes.

Can also be made in the top of a double boiler over boiling water. To avoid a skin on top, keep covered until used.

CURRY SAUCE

To basic white sauce recipe, add 1 tsp (5 mL) curry powder. For a little more bite, add 1/2 tsp (2 mL) ground ginger and a few grains of paprika or cayenne.

Using a small can (4 oz or 113 mL) chicken, heat chicken chunks in sauce.

Serve hot over toast. Garnish with parsley or paprika.

CHEESE SAUCE

Add 1/4 cup (50 mL) grated hard cheddar or mozzarella to white sauce. Heat slowly so cheese will melt without becoming rubbery.

Serve over steamed vegetables or cooked noodles. Garnish with parsley or paprika.

FONDUES ~~~~~~~~~~~~~~~~~~~~~~~~~~~~~

Unexpected company - and either you don't have enough plates or you simply don't feel like ruining a perfect sunset with a stack of dirty dishes. No problem.

Make cheese fondue. (You don't need the fancy pot and official fondue forks to have a good time.) For the vegetarians in the crowd - or just because - make a vegetarian fondue. For dessert, offer chocolate fondue with fresh fruit, marshmallows, plain cookies, graham wafers and nuts.

On the other hand, maybe the best fondues are for two.

CHEESE FONDUE

1 lb (454 g) cheese, well aged sharp Swiss or Cheddar	1 tbsp (15 mL) flour
3/4 cup (175 mL) dry white wine	chunks of bread, carrot and celery sticks, cauliflower and broccoli flowerets

146

Grate or slice cheese. In a paper or plastic bag, shake the cheese with the flour.

Mix cheese and wine in a double boiler or a heavy bottomed pot over a wire rack or asbestos mat on a stove top element. Heat until the cheese melts, stirring constantly. Remove from heat.

Skewer chunks of bread or vegetables onto forks or wooden skewers. Dip into hot fondue. If fondue begins to thicken, heat for a few more minutes.

SOBER CHEESE FONDUE

Fond of fondue but not fond of wine? Use this variation.

In place of wine, combine 3 tbsp (15 mL) butter or margarine and 1 tsp (5 mL) Worcestershire sauce. Treat as in recipe for Cheese Fondue.

QUICKIE CHEESE FONDUE

1 cup (250 mL) evaporated
  milk, undiluted
1/4 tsp (1 mL) salt
1 tsp (5 mL) dry mustard
few grains cayenne pepper

2 cups (500 mL) cheese, grated
  sharp or mild cheddar or
  mozzarella
chunks of brown or white
  bread for dipping

Put the milk and seasonings in the top of a double boiler over boiling water. Heat gently to simmering. Do not boil. When hot, remove from stove. Add cheese. Stir well, cover, let sit for 5 to 10 minutes or until cheese is all melted.

Serve with chunks of bread for dipping. Wooden skewers or salad forks will serve in place of proper fondue forks.

VEGETABLE FONDUE

1 cup (250 mL) olive oil
1 or 2 buds garlic, crushed
salt and freshly ground black
  pepper to taste

carrot and celery sticks,
  cherry tomatoes,
  cauliflower and broccoli
  flowerets, mushrooms

Heat olive oil and garlic in heavy-bottomed pot until gentle bubbles form. Add salt and pepper.

Use wooden skewers or forks to dip vegetables into hot oil to cook. Re-heat oil as necessary.

CHOCOLATE FONDUE

1 package Bakers semi-sweet
  chocolate, or chocolate
  chips
3/4 cup (175 mL) evaporated
  milk, undiluted, or whipping
  cream

1 tsp (5 mL) vanilla
strawberries, orange sections,
  apple slices, marshmallows,
  plain cookies, graham
  crackers, pecans, walnuts,
  pecans

Be careful that no water makes contact with chocolate, or mixture will simply go hard and unworkable. If this happens, add a little oil, heat, and it should soften.

Mix shredded chocolate or chips and milk or cream. Melt in double boiler or in pot with heavy bottom. Stir until smooth, remove from heat, add vanilla and stir.

Use fork or skewers or fingers to dip fruit, nuts, biscuits or cookies into melted chocolate. Re-heat if the chocolate mix gets too thick.

FRUIT DESSERTS ~~~~~~~~~~~~~~~~~~~~~~~~

PINEAPPLE DELIGHT

I shall ever be beholden to a Montreal-based friend for this recipe. Decorated with candles, it has been a successful birthday un-cake that was more sought after than the real thing. If you are planning to have on-board company in the evening, make this in the afternoon.

1 very ripe pineapple	1 box fresh strawberries
	toothpicks

Cut the pineapple in half lengthwise, cutting through the leaves and leaving them in place as decoration. With a sharp knife, cut away the core. Carefully cut the pulp away from the rind, keeping it in one piece. (You'll get better with practice.) Cut the pulp into cubes and fit back into the shell.

Clean and hull the strawberries and cut in halves or quarters. Using a toothpick, skewer a piece of strawberry, cut side down, into each pineapple cube.

Cover loosely with tin foil. Let stand for several hours to let the strawberry juice bleed down into the pineapple.

After your guests have devoured all the cubes, give the brave ones a spoon each and invite them to attack the shell, taking polite turns, of course. (It's worth the work - and the potential bath. The best of the strawberry-soaked pineapple juice is in the shell.)

MELON SALAD

The elusive taste is the "just a whiff" of freshly grated nutmeg.

2 oranges, peeled
1/2 tsp (2 mL) freshly grated
  nutmeg

1 cantaloupe
1 honeydew melon
2 kiwi fruit, peeled, sliced

Separate oranges into segments. Over a medium-sized bowl, cut each segment in half, adding all the juice. Sprinkle with freshly grated nutmeg. Halve melons, discarding seeds and centre pith. Scoop out and dice melon. Add melons and kiwi to oranges. Stir, set aside for a while to combine flavours. Even using the smallest available melons, this will serve 4 or 5 generously. Also, it will keep overnight to become a simple answer to breakfast.

EASY LUXURY STRAWBERRIES

1 small box strawberries
1 small carton of cream

1/2 cup (125 mL) white sugar

Clean and wash strawberries carefully, without removing the stems. Put the cream in a shallow little bowl. Stem and slice the imperfect berries and add to the cream. Set the perfect berries upright in the cream and leave until just before dinner.

    Roll each perfect berry in sugar. Ladle out the berries and cream into bowls, setting the perfect berries on top to be eaten with fingers. Have a napkin or two handy.

ROBIN'S FRUIT SALAD

This fruit salad was invented for our friend Robin, who is hypo-glycemic and can't have added sugar. It became so popular that we ate it even when Robin wasn't coming to dinner. It was also the answer to a pile of fruit that had reached its peak.

    Except for the oranges, pineapple and lemon juice, every-thing is exchangeable. The orange and lemon juice keeps the other fruit from going brown and the pineapple juice is a natu-ral sweetener.

2 oranges
1 apple
2 nectarines
few drops lemon juice
  concentrate

2-3 kiwi fruit
2 plums
med. can pineapple chunks
  in juice
small handful unsalted
  cashews or pecans

Peel oranges and chop over a bowl to save all the juice. Wash apple and nectarines, core and peel. Slice and add to the oranges. Squirt with lemon. Stir and leave for a few minutes. Peel kiwi fruit and slice. Add with pitted, sliced plums. Add canned pineapple and juice. Set aside to combine flavours.

    Sprinkle nuts over portions just before serving.

STEAMED APPLES

A warm and satisfying dessert to eat in the cockpit while you watch the setting sun spreading patterns across gently moving water.

1 apple per serving
1 tsp (5 mL) margarine per
  apple
2 tsp -1 tbsp (10-15 mL)
  brown sugar per apple

1/2 tsp (2 mL) cinnamon
  per apple
very small handful raisins
1/2 cup (125 mL) water

Core apples. Do not peel.

    Mix margarine, brown sugar and cinnamon into a paste. Add raisins. Stuff apple centres with mixture. Arrange on a rack in a pot with a tightly-fitting lid. Add just enough water to cover bottom of pot. Bring to boil. Cover and simmer at medium flame for 15 to 20 minutes or until apples are cooked. Cooking time will depend on type and condition of apples. Serve warm or cold with the pot liquid spooned over top of apples.

OOPS! STEWED FRUIT

And then I discovered that the apples, left to swing safely in their little string hammock, had been trying, unbeknownst to me, to beat themselves to death against the cabin wall. The resulting rescue became a dessert favourite. It will keep for a day or two - if you can keep Skipper or Crew out of the bowl.

2 oranges
2 apples
1/2 cup (125 mL) dates
1/2 cup (125 mL) dried
  prunes/figs
1/2 cup (125 mL) raisins

2 tbsp (30 mL) brown sugar
  (optional)
water: just enough to keep
  mixture from burning
1/2 tsp (2 mL) cinnamon
1/2 tsp (2 mL) nutmeg
1/2 tsp (2 mL) allspice

Peel oranges and apples. Core apples, dice. Chop oranges, dates, prunes and/or figs.

Add raisins, brown sugar if desired, and cook in heavy pot with spices and just enough water to keep fruit from scorching. Bring to a boil, then simmer over low heat, stirring frequently, until mixture is smooth and thick.

QUICK AND RICH ~~~~~~~~~~~~~~~~~~~~~

And every so often, the chocolate monster surfaces. Who said galley cooking should be conservative and health-conscious every minute of the time? In fact, who said that the satisfaction created by a good dose of chocolate just might *not* be emotionally nutritious? All these recipes are simple enough for kids to make but much too good to wait for them to do it.

FIVE-MINUTE FUDGE

This is absolutely the only fudge I can make successfully. All others either go grainy or never, never, never harden unless I freeze them. This stuff has never let me down. It's good, too.

2 tbsp (30 mL) margarine
2/3 cup (150 mL) evaporated milk
1-2/3 cups (400 mL) white sugar
2 cups (500 mL) marshmallows

1-1/2 cups (375 mL)
   chocolate chips
1/2 cup (125 mL) nuts,
   chopped (optional)

Mix margarine, milk and sugar in a heavy-bottomed pot over medium flame. Bring to a boil. Keep just simmering over medium flame for <u>exactly</u> 5 minutes, stirring constantly. Remove from heat. Add marshmallows and chocolate chips. Stir until marshmallows and chocolate melt. Add nuts. Pour into oiled pan. Cut into squares when cool.

CLUSTER CANDY

1 small bag chocolate chips
1 small bag butterscotch chips

1 can chow mein noodles
1/2 cup (125 mL) cashews or
   mixed nuts, chopped

Mix chips in a heavy-bottomed pan. Melt over low heat, stirring constantly. Remove from heat. Stir in chow mein noodles. Add nuts. Stir well. Drop by spoonfuls onto aluminum foil. Cool. • Use all chocolate or all butterscotch chips. • Use sesame seeds in place of nuts. • Add raisins.

DATE DROPS

This is a good activity for bored kids on a rainy day. The adults can help eat the results.

1 bag marshmallows
1-1/2 cups (375 mL) dates,
  chopped

2 cups (500 mL) nuts,
  unsalted, chopped
2-1/2 cups (750 mL) coconut

Melt marshmallows over low heat or in top of double boiler over boiling water. Add chopped dates and nuts. Mix well.

Put coconut in small bowl or cup. Drop spoonfuls of date mixture into cup and roll around until coated.

Variations: Roll in sesame seeds. • Use sunflower seeds rather than nuts. • Substitute Rice Krispies for the nuts and roll in finely chopped nuts rather than coconut. • Omit marshmallows. Chop or mash dates. Let kids squish them between clean fingers. Add chopped nuts and roll in sesame seeds for a more nutritious treat.

PUFFED RICE CANDY

"Soft ball stage" is reached when a drop or two of candy mixture, poured into a little saucer of cold water, can be gathered up in your fingers and formed into a soft little ball. Do not stop short of this process, or your candy will not set, ever, and the syrup part will leak through the rice and sit, limply, in the bottom of the pan. Yes, this is the voice of impatience speaking.

1/2 cup (125 mL) white sugar
1 cup (250 mL) corn syrup

1/4 cup (50 mL) water
6 cups (1.2 L) puffed rice
  cereal

Mix sugar, syrup and water in a large thick-bottomed pot. Cook over medium flame, stirring frequently, until the mixture reaches soft ball stage. Remove from heat. Pour into the cereal and stir hard until all the cereal is coated with candy mixture.

Oil a baking pan, cookie sheet or plate. Also oil your hands. Dump the candy mixture onto the pan or plate. Press flat with your finger tips. Cut into squares when cool.

PUFFED WHEAT CANDY

See Puffed Rice Candy for a definition of "soft ball stage."

1/2 cup (125 mL) margarine
1 cup (250 mL) brown sugar
2 tbsp (30 mL) cocoa
  (could substitute Ovaltine)

1/2 cup (125 mL) corn syrup
6 cups (1.2 L) puffed wheat
  cereal

Mix margarine, sugar, cocoa and corn syrup in heavy-bottomed large pot. Bring to a boil and cook over medium flame, stirring frequently, until mixture reaches soft ball stage.

Remove from heat. Add puffed wheat. Stir really well.

Oil a baking pan, plate or cookie sheet. Oil your finger tips. Drop candy mixture onto pan and press flat and smooth with fingers. Cut in squares when cool.

ONE-BY-FIVES

This is a perfect kids' treat. They can help make it, the ingredients are all "healthy," and it's so rich they won't want much.

Use equal amounts of each of 5 items. One cup (250 mL) is suggested.

1 cup (250 mL) peanut butter,
  plain or crunchy
1 cup (250 mL) liquid honey
1 cup (250 mL) dry powdered
  milk
1 cup (250 mL) raisins

1 cup (250 mL) unsalted nuts,
  chopped (Don't use peanuts
  for little tykes)
icing sugar, shredded coconut,
  sesame seeds or cereal for
  coating

Mix first five ingredients in order given. Form into spoon-sized balls.

Put icing sugar or coconut or sesame seeds or cereal into a cup or a bowl and have the kids roll the candy around in the coating.

Makes a couple of dozen little balls that are incredibly rich but do have some redeeming nutritional qualities.

RECEIPE INDEX ~~~~~~~~~~~~~~~~~~~~~~~~~

JOAN EYOLFSON CADHAM~~~~~~~~

A descendant of Icelanders, Joan Eyolfson Cadham grew up on a farm near Leslie, Saskatchewan. Attending a one-room country school, she was encouraged to love words and drama. Joan went on to earn a degree in Journalism, but writing was put on hold when she married and moved to Quebec. She raised her children, Inga, Ruthie and Joe and honourary son, Marc, while teaching in co-op nursery schools, then working with emotionally disturbed students in a residential treatment setting. Also, before such places were trendy, she was a partner in Le Quai, a tea/spice/natural foods store in Ste. Anne de Bellevue.

After she met Jack, there was something about working on *Hirondelle* with a man she wasn't sure she liked that sparked the creative spirit. Since then, writing has been her life, a fact much appreciated by her many readers.

After 26 years she left Quebec (and half her heart) and has returned to her home province. A journalist with some 4000 articles and several national column and provincial awards behind her, she lives in Foam Lake and writes for family-style magazines and several prairie newspapers. Her first book, written with Dennis Dwyer and David Letourneau, *Bent but not Broken, Today's Canadian Church*, was published in 1992.

SHORELINE ~~~~~~~~~~~~~~~~~~~~~~~~~~~~~~

Vi Bercovitch	Mirror, Mirror, *Terse Verse*
M. Laurel Buck	Stream of Memory, *Megantic County*
Joan Eyolfson Cadham	Red Right Returning
A. Margaret Caza	Walk Alone Together The Lights of Lancaster
Eugénie Doucet	Tapas, *A Spanish Interlude*
Dennis Dwyer	Beyond Jargon, *Mediation in Canada*
Dwyer, Cadham & Letourneau	Bent but not Broken, *Today's Canadian Church*
Judith Isherwood	Down to Earth A Walking Tour of Ste-Anne-de-Bellevue Tickets, *A Play in One Act*
Eve McBride	Dandelions Help
Sharen McDonald	A Gentleman and a Scholar
Neil McKenty	The Inside Story, *A former Jesuit priest*
Leslie Allison Minturn	Mildred Minturn, *A Biography*
Vera Gauley Munro	The September Years
Jerry Ray Nelson	Alaska Burning
Kathleen Regier	Connections, *Prairie Poetry*
Bess Burrows Rivett	Looking Back
Arnold Ruskell	Breaking the Ice, *An Arctic Odyssey*
Anna Woods	Healing Waters, *The Mayan Series*
Shulamis Yelin	Shulamis, *A Montreal Childhood*

AGMV
MARQUIS
Québec, Canada
1998